D1467047

IT'S TIME FOR YOUR COMEBACK

DON'T TAKE A STEP BACK WITH A SETBACK

TIM STOREY

Harrison House
Tulsa, Oklahoma

It's Time for Your Comeback
Don't Take a Step Back with a Setback
ISBN 1-57794-006-5
Copyright © 1998 by Tim Storey

Published by Harrison House, Inc.
P.O. Box 35035
Tulsa, Oklahoma 74153

Contents

IT'S TIME FOR YOUR COMEBACK

Dedication

To Isaiah and Chloe, my two children who bring laughter to my life.

INTRODUCTION

"The Pack is Back" topped the news headlines on January 27, 1997. The Green Bay Packers had won the Super Bowl for the first time in decades. The momentum of their comeback positioned the "Pack" for a "back-to-back" win in 1998. But football fans went wild when Denver Bronco's quarterback, John Elway, played the comeback game of his life in what was believed to be his final chance for a Super Bowl win before retirement, and took the coveted Super Bowl trophy home to Denver.

Everybody loves a comeback story. Abraham Lincoln ran for congress and lost, ran for the senate and lost, had a nervous breakdown and a troubled marriage; but he finally made it to the White House. George Foreman came back at forty-one years of age to become heavyweight champion of the world. Evander Holyfield,

Everybody loves a comeback story.

another world champion heavyweight boxer, had a serious health setback that threatened to end his career, but he came back to fight and win again. Moses, studying to be a great man of God, killed a man and ended up working at minimum wage for his father-in-law on the back side of the desert, but he came back and marched three million people out of Egypt. Joe Montana brought the San Francisco 49'ers back to victory. People love to cheer for the underdog. Look how many went to see Sylvester Stallone's *Rocky* movies. Rocky came back so many times he finally wore out his comeback in that last movie in '97!

> **Even while you are feeling the sting of your setback, your comeback is already being prepared for you.**

To be honest all of us experience setbacks in life at one point or another. Maybe as you are reading this, one of your children is in trouble or your finances are in crisis or your marriage is falling apart. Perhaps someone close to you is plagued by repeated setbacks, and you don't know how to help. Whatever caused you to pick up this book, I want you to know, *It's Time for Your Comeback*.

In the midst of a setback, people often take a step back. Then another setback comes, and they take another step back. Before long they find themselves so far from where they want to be they just give up. They can't see the light at the end of the tunnel, and they are overcome by the darkness. Life is doing something with them instead of them doing something with life.

If you are saying to yourself, "I've stepped back so far I don't even remember where I started from," just remember, no matter what took you off the yellow brick road, it's not how you start something, it's how you finish that counts. Even while you are feeling the sting of your setback, your comeback is already being prepared for you.

What do you envision for yourself in the coming year? I am offering you an opportunity for smooth sailing. By applying the solid principles in this book, you are going to sail over life's obstacles; and use these tools to raise the roof on your expectations — learn to dream again. Some of you have been living with four-foot ceilings when the sky is the limit.

I envision a comeback with your name on it. Your life has a purpose and an assignment. You were created to live by design not by default. You are being positioned to accomplish your destiny. When you come up against adversity, you will run right on through it without drowning or being burned.

Notice I didn't say "if" adversity comes, I said "when" adversity comes. You're probably asking, "Why do I have to go through the storms and trials?" Because somebody needs your test to turn into a testimony, and somebody needs your mess to turn into a message. Remember, someone worse off than you is always watching you. Let me show you how to become a power of influence and leave a legacy of encouragement and accomplishment for others to follow.

You may be at the point of giving up. You're weary and you don't know if you have the energy to start again. But listen to me, *It's Time for Your Comeback* so don't step back. It's too soon to give up. There is always time for one more comeback, and it's going to be a great one. Your limitations are your opportunities. You are a masterpiece in progress.

What I am sharing with you in these power-packed chapters are the truths and principles that have brought me through pain and desperation in my own life. It only takes ONE to change a life, and I am forever thankful for that ONE in my life who encouraged me and set an example for me to follow. Allow me to start you on the path to your comeback right now.

Don't put this book down until you make a commitment to set aside a specific time and place to finish reading it. Whether it is five minutes a day or an hour a day doesn't matter. Just do it! Read it again and again until you plant these principles and ideas in the depths of your heart. Your comeback is waiting for you!

CHAPTER 1

THE STORY OF A COMEBACK

D o you find yourself asking, "Is there more to life than what I'm living?" If so, rejoice that you are experiencing "divine dissatisfaction." You are being shaken out of complacency, out of your comfort zone, out of your "setback" mentality. Don't ignore what you are feeling. It's time to do a thorough housecleaning of all the junk in your life so that the unshakable essentials stand clear and uncluttered. It's time for your comeback.

Setbacks Happen

Setbacks happen to everyone time after time throughout life. There is no escaping it. You may have suffered so much pain and trauma that you have become numb to the injuries caused by the setbacks. You may not have laughed in a long time. You may be angry

> **Setbacks happen to everyone.**

because you've been abused, rejected, abandoned, stabbed in the back by a friend or family member, robbed or beaten.

A friend, who is a NFL linebacker, was hit so hard in a playoff game it broke his thumb. He was so caught up in the intensity of the game he didn't even know it was broken until eight plays later. His thumb was just dangling from his hand, and blood was everywhere when one of the other players noticed the injury.

My friend's adrenaline was so high he didn't feel the pain. That is the way you may be. You don't know you've been injured because you've been numbed by the trauma or else you're living life in the fast lane, and you haven't slowed down long enough to let yourself feel the pain.

Believe for Your Comeback

When you are in a setback, you have two choices:

- *sit in your setback,* or

- *believe for your comeback.*

Do you know how many times I wanted to quit, to just sit back in my setback and wallow in self-pity, because I was tired of all the cheap shots and battles?

Picture this. I'm walking through Dallas-Fort Worth Airport so tired my feet are dragging 10 steps behind me. This great motivator isn't feeling good at all. My hair's all whacked out. I've got my hat pulled down as far as it will go and my dark glasses on. I'm walking with my head down so I don't have to see or talk to anybody. I was in one of those "don't mess with me" moods. That's right, even "Mr. Encourager" has those kind of days. Not often, but I'm being real with you. It takes a lot to get me that way because I am up 98 percent of the time, but I was not feeling good that day.

A little lady comes running up to me calling, "Tim Storey, Tim Storey, Tim...." I'm thinking, "Oh no, not today." So I say, "Yeah?"

She says, "I don't want to bother you, but...." Then she proceeds to share a remarkable story saying, "You were at a church in Baton Rouge, Louisiana, and the place was packed to the rafters, over 6,500 people. I was sitting on the second row too weak to come forward, but your message and prayers became my light at the end of the tunnel when I was dying of cancer. Tim, that was three years ago. They gave me three weeks to live, and I'm not dead!"

What I want you to hear from this story is that in the midst of a setback people need hope. That's why you can't sit in your setback, because somebody needs you! I don't care how far you think you have sunk into the pit of despair, how desperately you have failed, how tragic your circumstances are or how badly you are hurting; somebody needs your testimony to help them get out of their desperate setback. And the best way to get out of your own setback is to reach out to help someone else. Why do you think so many support groups have sprung up all over the country – Mothers Against Drunk Drivers, Parents Who Have Lost Children, Alzheimer's Caregivers, etc.?

> ...the best way to get out of your own setback is to reach out to help someone else.

Turn Your Mess Into a Message

We're in the inner city of Los Angeles doing something we call,"Hope for L.A."A young crack dealer comes up for prayer. I watch him come up, and I see destiny inside all of that garbage on the outside. I say,"You, come here." His eyes are bloodshot. He's on crack. I say,"Why are you up here?"

Out of his heart he starts screaming,"I don't want to be a loser. I don't want to be a loser. You said I can be a winner. All my life I've been a loser." Tears began welling up in my eyes because I know what that feels like, to sit in a setback and cry,"Why, why, why...."

He's still screaming,"I don't want to be a loser!" His life was radically changed the moment he started following the message of hope and inspiration! He got free from the drugs. He started following us around to other meetings. We continued to teach him and helped him get out of his setback. Now he is helping other inner city kids who need the mess of his past life to be a message for them.

Different but Better

There's already a plan for your comeback that is greater than you could ever imagine. That plan is different than you may think because it holds a greater ultimate goal for your comeback. That's why your comeback is not what you expect it to be. It's even better.

Dave Dravecky was an All-Star pitcher with the San Francisco Giants when cancer was diagnosed in his pitching arm. Dave and his wife, Jan, were devastated and prayed to get through this unexpected, monumental setback. Following surgery the doctors told Dave, "Short of a miracle, you'll never pitch again."

Dave and Jan would not allow their faith to be shaken by this bad report. Dave fought back determined to make a comeback. Grueling physical therapy was required to train the other muscles in his arm to take over for the large deltoid muscle which had been removed with the tumor.

Within three months Dave rejoined the Giants in spring training. Returning to the pitching mound in his first game to the roar of the crowd cheering, "Welcome back, Dave," he bowed his head for a prayer of thanks and went on to pitch a winning game.

If you have heard Dave's story, you know his comeback was followed by another setback and then another and another. His pitching arm broke during the next game, and the cancer returned. Eventually his arm was amputated at the shoulder. Dave and Jan suffered through many physical and emotional losses, but they didn't allow themselves to sit in their setbacks.

> ...your comeback is not what you expect it to be. It's even better.

What they now know is that God was preparing a comeback that was very different from what they would have chosen or expected. Dave says, "Yes, I'd go through it all to get to where I am today. Because I know that through all of this I have become a better father, a better husband, a stronger Christian... just a better human being. God has changed me in ways I would have never thought possible."[1]

Return to Significance

I don't care where you are or how big a mess your life is, don't step back — God has your comeback already prepared. You may get tired of my saying this so often, but you must get this firmly planted in your heart. A comeback means to return to a place of significance, to return to a place of stature, to return to a place that was lost for a period of time. Sometimes we need to hear about other people's setbacks and comebacks so we can hold onto our own hope.

> **To come back means to return to a place of significance...**

Everyone messes up, even the great men and women in the Bible.

- Abram told his wife, Sarai, to lie and tell the pharaoh she was Abram's sister (Genesis 12:10-20), and yet God changed his name to Abraham and promised he would become the father of nations (Genesis 17).

- Moses let anger get the best of him and killed a man (Exodus 2:11-15), and yet he led the people of Israel out of Egypt (Exodus 12:31-42).

- Rahab was a prostitute, but she saved Joshua and Caleb (Joshua 2) and is listed in the lineage of David and Jesus (Matthew 1:6).

- Peter cut off a man's ear (John 18:10) and then denied Jesus (John 18:25-27). You know the other disciples must have thought, *Peter, get with it. We thought you'd get it once you cut off that man's ear. Now you're denying Jesus and cussing folks out by the fire.* God took away the shame, renewed Peter's name and let him preach on the day of Pentecost (Acts 2:14-47).

God did the same for all the others, and He'll do it for you too. So stop beating yourself up. See yourself and your faults and failures from a good father's point of view, from a God's eye view. God is a comeback kind of God.

> **God is a comeback kind of God.**

Beating the Odds

Evander Holyfield is quick to say, "There's no quit in me." It's that never-give-up attitude that has brought him back from two crushing defeats, making him a three-time heavyweight champion. He knows how to take a punch and come back for more. His grit is an inspiration to anyone who dreams impossible dreams.

In November, 1996, the betting odds were 25-1 against Holyfield winning over Mike Tyson. The sportswriters repeatedly wrote Holyfield was too small, too old and too nice to win again, predicting the fight wouldn't last three rounds.

At 215 pounds and thirty-four years of age, Holyfield entered the ring in Las Vegas as the underdog but he left the ring as a history maker with an 11th-round TKO. At that time his win against Mike Tyson made Holyfield only the second fighter to ever win three separate world heavyweight championships, the first being the great Muhammad Ali.

Here's what *Time Magazine* reported about the fight. "'I got caught in something strange,'" said Tyson. Or was it something wonderful, depending on your viewpoint. One of the sweetest men ever to practice boxing, Holyfield had won only two of his past four fights, and the Nevada Athletic Commission was so worried about a heart irregularity that it would not sanction the fight unless he received a clearance from the Mayo Clinic.

"'Nobody thought I could win,' Holyfield said. 'Their judgments were not based on our talents, [mine and Tyson's] though, but on our images. [We were pictured as] the monster with hate in his heart versus a man who was always talking about God. But the Bible tells us to have no fear, and I didn't. Besides, I've known Mike since I was seventeen. He's not so bad.'"[2]

You may ask why the odds were stacked so high against Evander Holyfield and how he did what everyone was saying he couldn't. Look at his record of inconsistencies:

- 1990 Holyfield won his first heavyweight championship against Buster Douglas and held his title until 1992, losing it to Riddick Bowe.
- 1993 in a rematch with Bowe, he won it back again.
- 1994 he lost his title to Michael Moorer. That same year Holyfield was diagnosed with a heart irregularity.
- 1995 Holyfield won over Ray Mercer with a decision.

In 1994 Evander met Janice Itson, M.D., who lived in Chicago. He was immediately impressed with her spiritual walk. A friendship flourished over long telephone conversations.

In October of '96 he had a conversation with God one day, and he called Janice and proposed. They were married in a simple ceremony in an Atlanta wedding chapel just a few weeks before the Tyson fight. There was no time for a honeymoon.

Holyfield had been training hard for months but things weren't going well. He was having trouble with his timing and with his rhythm. His sparring partners were getting the best of him. He shared his concerns with Janice early one morning on the phone.

She said to him, "You think God is not big enough to handle this problem." Then she began to sing this song, *I have made You too small in my eyes....* [3]

He finally got it. He was seeing God as small and his situation as being bigger than God. He kept singing that song over and over at practice and everything turned around. His timing and rhythm and speed came into line and his sparring partners were getting creamed.

Janice also played an important role in the last few hours before the fight at the MGM Grand Garden Arena. In their hotel room Evander admitted to Janice he was nervous, something he had never done before. Her response blew him away. They danced to the gospel song "Mighty Man of War," which got his focus off his nervousness and onto God.

> **God will preserve your life in order to preserve the purpose for your life.**

Walking out to the ring, in the ring before the fight and in his corner between rounds, his cornermen said, "Man, we can't understand you. What are you saying?" He said, "Don't worry about it. I'm not talking to you. I'm talking to God." [4] It was a history-making upset. God had already prepared his comeback.

Mercy to Cover Your Mess

Since then Evander has faced challenges in other arenas of life. But he refused to accept a setback. God's mercy is like no one else's, and so is His understanding. His mercy is powerful enough not only to cover all of your mess ups but also to change you in the process. He won't leave you the same or let you get away with the things you used to. God loves you too much, and He needs you. You are the only one He's got to do what He designed *you* to do. God will preserve your life in order to preserve the purpose for your life.

> When we let God take over and fulfill His purposes in us...the results are better than anything we can do.

Have you ever heard the saying, "Let go and let God"? When we let God take over and fulfill His purposes in us — according to His way and in His timing — the results are better than anything we can do. Let Him surprise you. He's going to rock your world and He may even shock you but I guarantee it will be good.

How Did I Get Here?

God can make your life so good, in fact you'll start having what I call how-did-I-get-here experiences. One of my first experiences of this kind came when I was in my early 20s.

I had been invited to Washington, D.C. to speak to the United States Congress on spiritual issues. As I stood in front of our nation's political leaders, I began thinking, "How did I get *here?"* Then, with a crack of the mallet, the Speaker of the House introduced me, "And now, the Honorable Reverend Tim Storey from Los Angeles, California." I stepped forward looking as honorable as I could and began my address.

That was an awesome experience for me, but I didn't get there on my own. I couldn't have. God prepared me and then He opened the door. That's how He works. He's been taking people from the pit to the palace for thousands of years. And if you're willing to go through His process, He'll take you too!

Your Daddy's a Winner!

Perhaps you're wondering why those how-did-I-get-here experiences are so important. The reason is simple. You were born to win. Your Daddy — God the Father — is a winner. And you were made in His image. So when you find yourself in a slump, remember, *it's only temporary.* God hasn't brought you this far to leave you.

Remember too, that you aren't the first person to experience a setback. God took me and countless others beyond failure and into success. And He'll do the same for you. You're not going to die a loser. You're going to do everything God put you on this earth to do.

CHAPTER 2

A MASTERPIECE IN PROGRESS

W hen you think about it, today is the first day of the rest of your life. You are a mighty person in the making, a masterpiece in progress, a miracle in motion; and nothing that has happened in the past can stop divine destiny for your life. God created you, and He's molding you into a vessel of honor for His purposes. He is breathing life into you to change you. You're not done yet, but you are headed for greatness.

No matter what you have lived through, what wrong decisions you have made, what challenges are staring you in the face, make a decision right now not to poison your future with the pain of the past. Your comeback is already prepared, and it's time to get ready for action. As you move through the chapters of this book and apply the principles you learn, you are going to be writing your own comeback story. The best part is we already know it has a happy ending.

Do you agree we can learn from the experiences of others? I do. Here's an incredible story of a guy who turned his mess into a message. Gideon lived in ancient days and his story can be found in the Bible in the book of Judges, chapter 6, but I'm going to bring it into today's language. It is amazing how a man's life lessons from thousands of years ago can be applied to you and your world.

An Unlikely Hero

Gideon was an unlikely hero, a simple man just trying to get by like so many of us until an angel tapped him on the shoulder and said, "You're the one. You're the man who's going to whip the Midianites off your turf. So, get ready, man. It's your time! And don't worry about a thing. You've got the BIG GUY on your side. He's with you all the way."

How did Gideon react? Just like many of us do when things aren't going our way, he was whining and complaining about his circumstances. He was cynical and skeptical and mad at God.

Here's what he said, "No way. If He's so great how come He let those Midianites invade our turf in the first place? Where's He been? Why are we going through all this stuff anyway? I heard about all the great things He did for everybody else years back. Why did He do it for them and not for us? As far as I'm concerned, He just checked out."

So many people feel that way about life. When they're in the middle of tough times, they immediately start asking the big "WHY" and blaming God for all their troubles. Does this sound familiar? "If God really loves me, why did He let my daddy leave? All my friends have daddies, why do I have to be different?" Or how about this one, "Why can't I be thin and beautiful like my best friend? God, it's not fair. She has all the fun, and everybody just laughs at me. I'm tired of this. I'll show them, I'm going to Dunkin Donuts and buy out the store."

Gideon was no exception. He was feeling sorry for himself, sitting in his setback — nursing, cursing and rehearsing his problems. Life was doing something with him instead of him doing something with life. What Gideon needed to do was release his problems to God, so God could reverse them. As long as we hang onto our problems and stay angry, God can't move in our behalf.

> **When God places a demand on your life or gives you a dream, He knows it's too big for you to do in your own might.**

Then Gideon did what so many of us do when we get an assignment, he started listing all of his limitations, the reasons why he couldn't do it. He said, "I can't do anything. My family's a mess. I'm a nobody. Those guys are bad dudes. Why do you think I'm hiding in this stinking wine cellar? Man, I can't even show my face on the street."

The angel ignored Gideon's whining and complaining and said, "Get over it. This is your big break. You can be 'the man' and save the day for your family and all your friends. Think how that's going to look on your resume. I'm telling you the BIG GUY is sending you, and He's given you everything you need to do it. Besides that, He'll be there, too. It's a piece of cake."

Don't Be Intimidated By Your Limitations

Our limitations don't intimidate God. He already knows what they are anyway, and He's big enough to change weaknesses into strengths. God doesn't overlook the obvious. He can do something with it to get you where you need to be.

God enjoys giving you a dream that's too big for you to do in your own might. God likes it when you dream big. In fact, a God idea is always something too big for you to do. He wants you to get excited and buy into His plan, but a God idea is always so huge, it causes you to feel awkward or overwhelmed enough to acknowledge that "it's going to take God" to do it.

Gideon could not imagine in his wildest dreams how he was going to drive out those mean Midianites who had been terrorizing the neighborhood. He didn't see himself as a "mighty man of valor," but God did. You may not be able to see yourself as a masterpiece, but God does.

In order for you to move out of your setback into your comeback, you have to understand how much God loves you. To do that you have to know Him as He is: compassionate, merciful, slow to anger, abounding in love. He doesn't point His finger at you and accuse you all the time or hold onto His anger. He knows all about your limitations, your obvious weaknesses, including your past wrongdoing, but He doesn't treat you as your actions deserve. He doesn't even remember them, so you don't have to drag all that junk from the past around with you anymore. It is forgotten as far as the east is from the west.

God Knows Your Frame

In fact, as high as the heavens are above the earth, that's how great His love is for you. God's love for you is absolute and unconditional. And, He knows your frame. The word "frame" means your form, your structure, your makeup, your fashion. It's the way you were put together. Each of us is unique and wonderfully made.

Somebody born and raised in a certain family in Stockholm, Sweden, is not the same as someone born and raised in a family in Compton, California. That's understandable. But when we join God's family, we think everybody is going to look alike, talk alike, act alike and walk to the same step. It doesn't happen because we're all coming from different perspectives and backgrounds.

You didn't come from where I came from, and I didn't come from where you came from. Perhaps you weren't raised in a happy childhood. Who knows the hell you may have gone through. It doesn't make sense to suddenly call you a Christian, put you in church and expect you to be perfect overnight. Your frame may be different from everyone else's.

So even if you are struggling, you can do something BIG. God is able to turn your life around to set you on top. That's not too hard for Him. I like to say it this way, God could walk *and* chew gum at the same time!

You are a masterpiece still in progress. You aren't done yet, but you're headed in the right direction. God is the potter and you are the clay. God is molding you into the person He wants you to be. It may not feel good right now, but you're on your way! When a potter is forming a pot on his wheel, it doesn't look perfect overnight, but it's on its way. God knows your form.

Let's look back at Gideon again. The angel says, "Man, I've got a God idea for you. Do something big here." Gideon states the obvious and says, "I wish I could, but I'm semi-retarded, my form is messed up."

The angel is thinking, *We can handle this. I'll just pull it up on the computer under* **www.semi-retarded people God has helped.com.** *Wow, look at that list: Abraham, Isaac, Jacob, Moses, Rahab...Yeah, we can handle him!*

The angel says to Gideon, "Listen, your weakness is going to turn to strength. You're a mighty man of valor, a mighty man in the making!"

Been There! Done That!

When God went to Moses with His God idea and Moses said, "God, I don't think You can handle me, I killed a man and I can't talk straight"; God said, "Been there! Done that! I am the God of Abraham, Isaac and Jacob. Check out My resume!" So when you think your obvious weakness is too big, look at the obvious weaknesses God has dealt with in people in the past and see how they made it.

> **You're going to be all right because God is on your side!**

All the promises of God for you are yea and amen. That's why your life is going to have a happy ending, whether you believe it or not right now. You're the head and not the tail. You're above and not beneath. You're going over and not under. And no weapon formed against you shall prosper! You're going to be all right because God is on your side! It has little to do with your ability, because when you are weak, He is strong.

Some of the greatest songs were written in the darkest hours. Some of the most powerful books came out of desperate times. Sometimes it takes a time in the pit before we finally look up and see God is there for us. We try to get out but we can't move forward or back or from side to side. The only way out is up, and that's where we bump right into God and all that He is: Provider, Healer, Good Shepherd, More than Enough.

It Takes All Kinds!

There are three kinds of people: the pessimist, the idealist and the realist. An idealist can be in the middle of a hellhole he created and think he's going to get out overnight. He's $300,000 in debt and watches a real estate infomercial and is convinced if he buys that real estate, he'll reverse the curse overnight. It isn't going to happen.

The idealist stays up late and watches all the infomercials. You know the ones that sell Ab-flexing gut-busters. He's as round as he is tall, sitting in his recliner, eating a triple-meat, extra-large pizza. He hollers to his wife, who is in bed trying to sleep, and says, "Baby, order that thing for me. Call the number right now, 1-800-GET-SKINNY!" He thinks it's going to hit him with "instant skinny" just like the commercial.

Another sure sign of an idealist is someone who always has a crazy slogan for everything. It's good to be optimistic and to think positive, but an idealist does not see reality. He oversimplifies problems and solutions.

Then there's the pessimist who always sees the dark side of things. There is a well-known book by Jonathan Swift called "Gulliver's Travels." Remember, Gulliver was a great big guy and the rest of them were little. No matter what happened to Gulliver, there was one little guy who always said, "We'll never make it!" Gulliver would say, "Man, we're going to get over this hill." The little guy was a pessimist.

Another identifying statement of a pessimist is, "Yes, but...." You're headed to the beach, and the sun is shining bright without a cloud in the sky, the pessimist will sit in the backseat saying, "Yes, but it's going to rain." He doesn't see the rainbow in the sky, all he sees are the rain clouds. A pessimist is often so into that negative state of mind, he won't let the light come in to change that type of attitude.

Now the realist sees the obvious but is willing to devise a plan to correct the problem. He says for example, "Yes, I made a mistake when I made that investment. I should have done more research. I don't plan on making that kind of decision again without having all the facts." He will look to find a solution. That is the position where we want to be.

A Night to Remember

I was a senior in high school, the prom was a week away, and I got a big pimple on the end of my nose. It wasn't just a regular pimple that goes away overnight, it was an acne cyst. These are huge, giant, ingrown, deep-seeded, master-planned pimples.

I was a waiter at a place called Jimmy's Restaurant, and my customers looked at me and said, "Whoa! Give that boy a tip!" I was real upset, and I was talking with some of the waitresses saying, "Man, the prom is in ten days, do you think this thing is going to go down?" It seemed like it just kept getting bigger and redder. One waitress said, "Oh, that's nothing! You can hardly see it! Just put a little bit of makeup on it!" She was an idealist.

The manager came by and said, "Man, Tim, what happened to you? That thing's huge!" I said, "You think it's gonna go away by next Friday?" Pessimist that he was, he said, "Not in a month of Sundays!"

I had this cute date for the prom, and I was in a panic. I solicited every remedy anyone could offer. You name it, I tried it. I was an idealist and I walked around all week saying, "It's gonna go down, it's gonna go down, it's gonna go down." One day before the prom, I was saying, "Mom, it's gonna go down. I just know it."

One of my relatives was visiting on vacation and she came up to me and said, "Somebody needs to get real with you, Tim. It's huge, and it's not going away overnight." She was a realist, stating the obvious, and saying, "You'd better deal with it and find some other solution, because you've got a big knot on your nose, and it's going to stay there."

Get Real

You may have some huge, obvious problems in your life. It may be the car you drive, it may be the body you're in. It could be your stamina because you're not in shape. It could be your health or your finances. Your marriage may be in trouble. It's time to get real. One reason we face so many dilemmas over and over and over and never pass go to collect our $200, like in Monopoly, is because we do not get real. We keep acting like our problem is going to go away, like someone's going to come wash your car while you're at work. No, that car is going to stay dirty unless you wash it or pay someone else to wash it. Get real!

Gideon was dealing with the obvious but God was saying to him, "I know your frame. I know what I've got to deal with. I am the Master Architect and I can handle this one!"

Hebrews 11 is a chapter in the Bible that talks about the faith and courage of many great men and women. As great as they were, they all had weaknesses, and their obvious ones weren't any different than yours and mine. But it says their weakness was turned to strength. The word "turned" means a slow, deliberate turn. That's hard for us Americans to swallow. We're the now generation. We don't want to wait for anything or anybody.

That's Growth

If the great men and women in the Bible had their weaknesses turned slowly to strengths, that means there was a growth process taking place. It didn't happen overnight for them and it won't for you that way either. If one of your weaknesses is being moody, maybe you were moody every day last year and now you're only moody every other day. That's growth. If you're just a little better each day or each week, eventually your weakness will become a strength. Don't focus on your weakness, *focus on your increasing strength.*

> **Don't focus on your weakness,** *focus on your increasing strength.*

I'm not talking to your mind, I'm talking to your spirit, your inner man, where your weakness is turning to strength. Whether your weakness is an addiction, a bad temper, poor work habits or whatever, by God's power that weakness is being turned to a strength. God keeps nudging you to keep growing one step at a time so you get better each day no matter how long it takes.

The book of Proverbs says a righteous person falls seven times but rises up again (Proverbs 24:16). Abraham Lincoln once told a friend, "I'm not so concerned you have fallen but that you rise."[1] You're going to shock yourself. Life gets good when you know you're changing. All of a sudden one day you're going to realize you're happy.

No Fishing Allowed

If you were raised in chaos, chaos became part of your frame and culture. So when you find yourself in peace and happiness, don't go back and play your past videos. That's how you sabotage your own victories. You're a new person. Just because everybody else is going through chaos and hell, doesn't mean you have to participate.

Old relationships will try to wrap their form around you and pull you back into your old ways of living. Don't let it happen. God is going to start rearranging your friends and putting you with people who understand you're not the old you. You're not locked in your old form. You're going to have a whole lot more respect for yourself when you start seeing yourself from a God's eye view. God doesn't go fishing in your past, so you need to hang up your fishing pole, too.

Big Waves Happen

In the midst of your obvious obstacles, God is challenging you to do big things. You have a purpose, a God idea to fulfill. Opposition is going to happen so expect it and deal with it.

Opposition is going to happen so expect it and deal with it.

I was bodysurfing in Hawaii on a sandy beach. Picture me with this big Afro, bodysurfing with all the locals. The waves were big and I wasn't used to the currents and undertow. A wave would hit and knock me down. I'd try to get up and another wave would come and hit me again and again and again. Finally, it pulled my swimsuit clean off me. I had to swim around and find my swimsuit before I could go to shore, all the while still being hit with those big waves.

Life seems that way sometimes, doesn't it? You get hit and get back up. BAM! You get hit again. BAM! Something else hits. Knocks your drawers off! Now you've got to chase down your drawers while the waves keep hitting. You feel like saying, "Stop already, just leave me alone! I don't want to change. I like 'me' just the way I am." But you're not a person who is just going to barely get by. You're a trailblazer, a world shaker and a history maker. You'll encounter obstacles and opposition and the pain of setbacks, but you're coming out of it all.

Even while you're feeling the sting of a setback — the sting of "I can't believe I have cancer," the sting of "I can't believe he left me," the sting of "I should have gotten that job" — there's a comeback plan already being orchestrated. God is getting you ready, preparing you for your comeback right now. If you are plugged into God, He is creating somebody different inside of you, making you into the person He wants you to be.

Hot Pants

Years ago back when we were "poh" (that means poorer than poor), my sister and I were invited to Miami by some very nice people who had a big yacht. It was hot and the only nice pair of pants I had were made of thick wool.

I had never worn these pants before, and they had never been hemmed, so I had to tape them up. It was 103 degrees on a yacht in Miami, my wool pants were hemmed with masking tape, and I was sweltering. I was trying to act normal and enjoy myself when all of a sudden I felt my pants start to unravel. You've got to understand this wasn't just a small cuff. Those pants had been made for Shaq O'Neal not skinny, little Tim Storey. There was a lot of pant leg and a lot of tape hanging out when it all let loose. I slid over to my sister and whispered, "Quick, go get the masking tape out of the car and meet me in the bedroom!" My frame was being exposed.

That's how life is sometimes, stuff just starts falling everywhere. Your frame is being exposed. Pressure squeezes it out and you feel like you're breaking. It stings. That's when it's time to let the Master Architect step in.

Words Have Life

You can change your environment by the words you speak. Stop talking about your weaknesses and start talking about your strengths. Life and death are in the power of the tongue. I like to say it this way, "You'll never reach the palace by talking like a peasant." Get your mind off what you don't have and onto what you do have. Look at what Christopher Reeve is doing with what he still has.

Christopher Reeve is truly a "super man" in my opinion. After the terrible riding accident that left him paralyzed and breathing on a respirator, he questioned the value of his life and considered if it would be better for everyone if he just died. He mouthed these words to his wife, Dana, "Maybe we should let me go." She said, "I will support whatever you want to do because this is your life and your decision. But I want you to know that I'll be with you for the long haul, no matter what. You're still *you* and I love you."[2]

Her words framed his decision not to step back from life in the midst of what appeared to be a devastating setback. Yes, he is still paralyzed, but he hasn't sat still for a moment. He has fought his way through this setback and is working with researchers around the world to develop a solution for spinal cord injuries. He believes in the face of the impossible that a solution will be found in his lifetime. We've seen him in the political arena and helping charities. Recently he published a book titled, *It's Still Me*, coined from Dana's powerful words.

> **When you believe what *God* says about your situation, you will begin to change what *you* say...**

Here's a revelation you need to get in your spirit and your heart. When you believe what *God* says about your situation, you will begin to change what *you* say about it. Believe that God can do what He said He would do. He has quite a track record after all. He made the heavens and the earth (Genesis 1:1). He gave a 100-year-old man a son (Genesis 21:1-3). He parted the Red Sea (Exodus 14). He calmed the stormy sea and walked on the water (Matthew 14:25). He heals the sick and opens blind eyes (Matthew 15:30). He has a mansion prepared for you in heaven (John 14:2). Don't you think if He has done all that, He can do what He has told you He will do?

If you don't know how to believe what you can't see with your natural eyes, get around somebody who dares to believe the impossible and has the courage to see the invisible. Link yourself to a world shaker, hang around with a history maker and a risk taker. Stick with people who will keep telling you "everything's going to be all right." Their faith and positive belief system will get inside of you. Fill your tank with the right kind of fuel. Plug in to people who will wake you up, stir you up, help you up and shake you up. Find someone who has life inside them. They are contagious.

There is power in your words. As you begin to believe what God said, it will change what you say, because out of the abundance of the heart, the mouth speaks. God is big. Fill your insides with Him and you'll start talking and believing like Him: Big. "Man, I've been through hell,

> **Fill your insides with Him and you'll start talking and believing like Him.**

but I'm going to get a breakthrough." "I should have gotten that job, but I'm going to get the next one." "I don't know why that knuckle-head left me, but God's got someone better for me." It takes effort but it's worth it when you see you're obviously changing.

Keep Moving Forward

Success not only takes effort, it also takes time. That's why in the midst of the setbacks, the opposition and the limitations, you must keep moving forward. Don't pause along the way to recount past failures, to indulge in self-pity or to yield to negative talk. Stay focused on your journey. Remember the key is progress.

You aren't the first to embark on such a pathway and you aren't walking it alone. God is with you to refresh and revitalize you. He will give you a vision for a future that is better than anything you have yet dreamed. Allow Him to strengthen and guide you into the comeback He has already prepared.

CHAPTER 3

STAYING STEADY IN UNSTEADY TIMES

H as your life or that of your family been torn apart by drugs or alcohol addiction? Do you have all that money can buy but still feel empty and useless? Have you struggled and sacrificed to climb the ladder of success only to have the words "buy-out" and "downsizing" cut the ladder rungs right out from under your feet? Have your dreams been smashed on the highway of defeat? Whatever your setback is, don't take a step back because God has already prepared your comeback. No matter how unsteady your life appears to be, stay steady.

Don't Give Up

This isn't the time to give up no matter what is happening around you or to you. During the terrible storms created by El Niño in 1998, a devastating tornado hit a southern community. In a TV news interview a third grader who had huddled with her classmates in the elementary school hallway as the funnel cloud roared overhead was asked if she was afraid. She replied matter of factly, "No, I just cried and prayed to Jesus!" No one at the school was injured. What an awesome testimony of what it means to stay steady during unsteady or turbulent times.

> **When life takes on the appearance of a battlefield, we must learn to fight and press on through to victory.**

When life takes on the appearance of a battlefield, we must learn to fight and press on through to victory. Don't get discouraged. You aren't alone, and you aren't the first person to go through such a battle. Look at what others before you have done.

Led By Example

In the Bible the apostle Paul set an example for others, such as young Timothy, to follow. Paul readily displayed his own faults presenting himself as a most unlikely candidate to be chosen for service, admitting he had been a #1 public enemy with no credentials of his own for a comeback.

Timothy, who had been called to be a world shaker and a history maker, was facing a difficult trial. He was in a setback. There was an economic and spiritual famine in his country. All hell was coming against his life. Paul encouraged him to remember the promise that he was going to be an example in his youth. Paul told him to hold on to that promise and fight for it.

Timothy was destined to be a great leader even though he came from a dysfunctional family. His mother and grandmother were godly women, but his father was another story. Most of the time Timothy did very well, but every once in awhile he would lean a bit and think about giving up.

Paul cautioned him not to take a step back saying, "Listen, Timothy. I know what you're talking about because I messed up big time, but God enabled me to do what I'm doing now."

I looked up the word "enabled" and it means "to supply with means, knowledge or power — to make possible."[1] So, when God enables you, He gives you *everything* you need to carry out the divine plan for your life.

Paul continued saying, "I know what it's like to feel like giving up, but don't do it. Hold on and keep fighting. So there's famine in the land. Go ahead and admit it. But Timothy, you've got to take your eyes off the circumstances and realize you don't have to participate in the famine!"

America in Famine

I believe there is a famine in America. In fact America is going semi-crazy. When a basketball player is paid 98 million dollars a year to play for seven years in the NBA and inner-city schoolteachers are only being paid $18,000 a year, something is terribly wrong. Priorities and values are all out of whack.

That's why America is in famine. People are living discouraged, depressed lives. Families are disintegrating. Children are killing their own teachers and classmates. Natural disasters are destroying fertile farmland and devastating cities and coastlines.

America is reaping what has been sown. When the wrong seeds are sown, the wrong harvest comes forth. The principle of sowing and reaping has a boomerang effect. When you throw a boomerang, watch out, or it will come back and hit you on the side of your head. Did you ever hear one of your parents say, "What goes around comes around?"

Yes, there is a famine, and much of America is reaping the effects, but you can choose not to participate. Make this your confession instead: "I am standing on the promises of God. I am living steady, walking steady, remaining steady in unsteady times. I choose not to be broke. I choose not to live in poverty. I choose not to walk in discouragement. I choose to walk God's way."

Feast on His Promises

In the midst of a famine we need to feast on God's promises. The Bible is filled with hundreds of promises that belong to all generations and apply to every aspect of daily living; such as faithfulness, hope, joy and happiness, talents and giftings, success, marriage and family, protection and security, promotion, guidance, knowledge and wisdom. The list goes on and on. Sometimes called blessings or benefits, these promises are available to all who choose to live according to God's principles.

> **In the midst of a famine we need to feast on God's promises.**

I believe God has specific promises for you that relate directly to His purpose for your life — financial security, good health, providing a godly spouse, restoring your family relationships, giving you a child. Whatever your purpose, your dream, your vision, there is a promise to meet your need in fulfilling it. So embrace it as yours.

Armed With Hope

In 1993 at the age of twenty-two John Foppe was selected as one of the Ten Outstanding Young Americans. Previous award winners included Presidents Kennedy, Nixon, Ford and Clinton, as well as Vice President Albert Gore and astronaut Dr. Kathryn Sullivan. In his acceptance speech this is what John shared with the audience: "When my brother learned I was to receive this honor and saw a picture of the trophy with two silver hands reaching to touch each other, he told me, 'John, you're finally getting just what you've always needed — your very own pair of hands.'" Waves of laughter and applause filled the ballroom attesting to the impact of this young motivational speaker.

You see, John Foppe was born without arms and with a number of other serious birth defects. Doctors told his parents he had a one in a million chance to survive, but he overcame the odds. Then they said he would never walk, but at the age of two John took his first steps toward independence.

John's remarkable positive attitude is reflected when he shares how as a child he bitterly asked God, "Why me?" The response he got was, "John, why *not* you?" At that point John knew that God had a significant purpose for his life, and the promise he held onto was hope for a fulfilling future.

The pain and struggles John has endured and overcome seem insurmountable in the natural. Born without arms, he does everything with his feet, including dressing himself, driving a car, writing, cooking and eating. Through it all, John determined that the only real handicaps are those mental and emotional ones which prevent us from fully participating in life. In the face of every struggle and setback of which there have been many, John has held onto his promise — hope — and now is fulfilling his purpose of encouraging and helping others as he speaks to thousands in schools and businesses across America.

No matter what external or internal pressures come against you, hold on to your promise. External pressure comes from the forces of evil in the world. Internal pressure comes from within when you cause your own problems by the way you think or the choices you make because of things from your culture or your past.

How many times do things happen in our life and our immediate reaction is to say somebody else did it? Back in the '70s comedian Flip Wilson portrayed a character named Geraldine on his TV show. No matter what happened Geraldine's answer was always the same, "The devil made me do it!" In real-life setbacks, many times the devil didn't have anything to do with it and neither did anyone else — we did it!

I've been going to Nacho's Barber Shop to get my hair cut since I was ten years old. One day as I pulled up in front of his shop, I thought I'd put my car in park when actually I'd put it in reverse. I reached down to get my wallet, and I felt something go "Bam!" I jolted back up in the seat and said, "Somebody hit me!" I was mad and started looking around saying, "Somebody's stupid. Who hit me?" I got out of my car, and here's this beat up old Celica behind me. Nobody was in it so I'm thinking, "This was a hit and run."

A lady who lives next door to Nacho's came out of her house. She said, "I saw it." I said, "Well, what did he look like?" She said, "You hit it." I said, "You're teasing." She said, "No, you hit it." I had to go into Nacho's Barber Shop and get the man out and say, "I hit your car." I had to go to my car insurance agent and say, "I hit the car." It was weird to have to admit, "I hit the car." That's the way it is in life sometimes. Our setbacks can be caused by our own actions. The quicker we are to get real and tell ourselves the truth, the better off we'll be.

Don't be discouraged when the circumstances in your life don't add up to God's promises. When the highway of life is bumpy and filled with potholes, sometimes all you have is a promise. Be nourished and encouraged by it. Hold on to it. God will not lie.

> **The battle is always the fiercest just before the victory.**

Get a new fight in your spirit. Say this to yourself over and over until you believe it, "I'm not going to live a mediocre lifestyle. I'm not going to barely get by the way some of my relatives have done. I believe all of the promises of God are yes and will come to pass in my life. I am going to have a great life just like the Bible says I can. My family is going to come to God. My breakthrough is here!"

Understand this: The battle is always the fiercest just before the victory. Right before your financial breakthrough or right before great things are about to happen in your life, you may feel like all hell has broken loose. That's why you must be prepared to stay steady. Don't give up too soon. Just hold on.

Tenacity of a Pit Bull

I was watching the David Letterman show, and one segment of the show was about pet tricks. They brought a big tree into the studio, and a pit bull dog jumped up and ripped the limbs off one at a time. It was something to watch. Then he got to one big branch that he couldn't rip off, but he wouldn't let go. His jaws were locked. He growled and ripped and tore at that branch. The audience went wild. That dog would not let go of that branch until he pried it loose. That's how we need to be in reaching for our promise. We need to latch on and not let go no matter what comes against us.

> ...don't get distracted by what other people are going through or what they are saying about your life.

In the midst of all the craziness in this world, don't get distracted by what other people are going through or what they are saying about your life. Have you ever seen a horse in a race wearing blinders on both eyes? That is so he won't get distracted by the horses on either side. He focuses on the race and getting across the finish line. If you keep your focus on the finish line of your comeback, you won't be distracted by circumstances, by other people or by anything going on around you.

Battle Techniques

When you're in a battle, here are four things to do:

(1) *Start affirming people in a bigger way.* When you're feeling down, start saying something positive to somebody, speak big, stir somebody up, speak life into someone, shove it inside of them. And it doesn't hurt to speak positive affirmations to yourself as well.

(2) *Press the battle.* That means be aggressive and run toward the battle not away from it. It puts you on the offensive

rather than the defensive. Young David ran toward Goliath. Did you ever wonder why all battle armor was worn on the front of the body? It's because you can't win a battle running away.

(3) *Believe bigger.* If one dream dies, believe for a bigger one. When circumstances seem impossible, believe bigger, reach higher. Set new goals. Surround yourself with dream seekers and world shakers.

When you're pushed into a corner, dream yourself out of it. Some of our greatest dreams come out of such corners. Out of all the hard times, setbacks, discouragement and cheap shots I've experienced, I saw myself touching Washington, D.C. I saw myself impacting celebrities and professional athletes. I dreamed bigger than even I could imagine.

(4) *Pray bigger, harder and stronger.* Get out of your depression for five minutes and pray intense prayers. Put pictures of your family members in front of you and pray over them. Pray the kind of enough-is-enough prayers that will move the mountains out of their lives. Refuse to cower or step back anymore. Remember, these days are intense, and the battle is fierce. You can't allow yourself to be lulled into a false sense of security. You must be aggressive. Charge forward with everything you've got, and you'll discover that persistence will break the resistance.

Hold Your Ground

God has put all of His power at your disposal. And you have a right to use that power to get through any and every setback you face. You also have an obligation to clear the way for future generations. It's your responsibility to leave a legacy of faith.

Begin to forge that legacy by discovering the promises that God has given you in His Word. As you learn about His benefits, refuse to let go of them no matter what storms may come. Refuse to blame others for your setbacks. Refuse to believe ideas and opinions that oppose the Word of God. Learn how to believe God's Word even when you can't see it with your own eyes. His Word is the truth. And that truth can change all of the facts!

That's why you must never give up. God has said you are going to make it, and therefore, you are! So go ahead and visualize your comeback. God has already prepared it for you.

CHAPTER 4

A PAVED PATHWAY

D o you have a hard time comprehending how BIG God is? Don't feel bad if you answered yes. In our small human minds we are limited by the here and now, by what we can see with our eyes and hear with our ears. Somehow we don't have any problem exaggerating the greatness of some humans we call heroes — the sports legends, the rock musicians, the war generals, the movie stars — yet, we can't believe God is big enough to lift us up out of our setbacks.

I was walking through the airport one day with Charlton Heston, and I was amazed at the response he still gets from having played Moses in the movie, *The Ten Commandments*. People were actually walking by saying, "There's Moses." I asked him, "What is the weirdest response you've ever received?"

He said, "Well, I was in the Holy Land a couple of years ago filming when a busload of people from Asia came along. They saw me talking and thought Moses had come back. They ran off the bus all excited about seeing Moses."

If Charlton Heston creates that kind of response because he played Moses, how much more should we respond to *God?* After all He is the great I AM. He is the God Who is more than enough. He is a BIG God, and He has BIG plans for you.

God wants to take you to another level in your life.

God wants to take you to another level in your life. The only way this can happen is if you allow Him to change you into His image and take you from glory to glory which means from transition to transition. You see, God is a living, personal presence, not a piece of chiseled stone. And when God is personally present, there is nothing between us and Him. Our faces will shine with the brightness of His face. As we allow Him to change us, our lives become brighter and more beautiful, and we become more like Him. Now that's exciting! God wants to take you to a new level in your family, your spiritual walk, your finances, your dreams and your comebacks.

Are you ready to go from glory to glory? He has already paved a pathway for you and made it smooth. Now that doesn't mean it's going to be easy, and it may not be as you expect it to be. He may even ask you to do something that doesn't make sense. The key is obedience.

When God has a plan, He knows the end from the beginning. Often there is more to the story than meets the eye, and He needs us to follow His instructions to the letter. It may be a matter of life and death.

When Saul (who later became the apostle Paul) was blinded on the road to Damascus, he knew he had encountered the living God (Acts 9). Saul was well-known for his zealousness in tracking down Christians — both men and women — and having them killed. He was feared in the Christian community. So Ananias was flabbergasted when God told him to go pray for Saul.

You Want me To Do What?

To Ananias it made no sense to endanger himself by going to find Saul. He had heard what sort of man this was. Here Ananias is about eighty years of age in his retirement years. He's relaxed in life, probably playing golf twice a week. He has his favorite TV shows down pat, his favorite charities. He's part of the country club and Promise Keepers. Then along comes God with this tough assignment.

Imagine what was going on in his mind. He probably said, "It's bad enough, You disturbing me at my age for such a job, and now You're giving a murderer visions of me!" And being as human as you or me, Ananias tried to talk God out of it! But God knew the rest of the story, and He demanded obedience.

You see, God had a plan for Saul that was greater than anyone could imagine. He knew that as zealous as Saul was in his beliefs, he would be a mighty servant for His kingdom. Saul was a man who could not be compromised.

God also had a plan for Ananias, and it was critical that he obey and do exactly what he was told to do no matter how dangerous it appeared to be. Who could have ever imagined the impact Saul of Tarsus would have on generations to come? What if Ananias had not been obedient? Thirteen books of the Bible might never have been written.

Prepare for the Unexpected

You need to understand what it was like for Ananias because God may require the same from you. You'll be going along minding your own business, and suddenly God will do something big in your life. It may not make any sense, and it may even seem dangerous. But if it's a God idea, it's going to happen, so prepare for the unexpected because it's coming.

Just think how you would respond if I said to you, "Last week I led Charles Manson to the Lord, and he was baptized. I know he's done some bad things, but he's a changed man. They've let him out of prison, and he's out in the car. He needs a place to stay for a few days. Could you put him up in your guest room?"

Would you wonder, "Is this for real? Surely God wouldn't want me to endanger my home and family by taking in a convicted murderer."

The point is God's ways are not our ways, and He has an imagination that outdoes even Steven Spielberg's special effects or James Cameron, the director of the *Titanic*. You can't imagine what God has been dreaming up for you to do in these critical days ahead.

Get in Shape

From the beginning of time, the Lord has been saying, "Get yourself in shape, deal with your character, attack the little foxes that spoil the vine." He wants us to take care of the little things that would hinder us, so we can make room for the big assignments He has for us! He is ready to give you a God idea, to give you a purpose. It is up to you to be prepared to carry it out.

Change Is Guaranteed

I mentioned earlier that going from transition to transition means change is guaranteed. The pathway you have walked in the past may be very different from where you will walk in the future. He is going to stretch you and expand your horizons. God is raising the roof, so start thinking like God thinks. It's not about maintaining the status quo saying, "My daddy never made more than $20,000 a year so I can't expect anything better." It's about raising the roof, blowing the ceiling off and believing God will supply all of your needs.

> **The pathway you have walked in the past may be very different from where you will walk in the future.**

God has already paved the pathway of your assignment. He just needs your cooperation. Just as He paved the way for Ananias by giving Saul a dream that he would come and pray for him, He has made a way for you. When trials come, He will smooth out those problems and difficult areas in your life. Even as you read this, Jesus is personally praying for you — making intercession for you at the right hand of the Father (Hebrews 7:25). Warring angels are doing battle for you in the heavenlies.

So a pathway has already been smoothed. Are you ready to walk down it? Many people won't do it because they are caught up in their own routine. They are in a rut. How many times have you heard someone say, "This is the way I've always done it"? In more modern business terms they say, "If it works, don't break it". God is looking for people who will think differently, who are willing to break the mold and start over.

General George Patton is one of my favorite military heroes. He had the guts to stand up for what he believed and his aggressive combat strategy played a key role in the headlong Allied armored thrust into Germany after D-Day in World War II. In the summer of 1944 he commanded the Third Army which broke through the German defenses in the Normandy campaign quickly moving across France. In March 1945 his army crossed the Rhine River into Germany and moved toward Austria. Patton's bold and flamboyant personality quirks were controversial, but he was a man who thought outside the mold and got the job done at a time when the world was in turmoil.[1]

> **Break the mold of your past. Take a risk and do something you've never done before.**

In these times that's what God is looking for from us — the guts to think outside the mold and do things differently if that's what it takes to get the job done. Dare to be different. Break the mold of your past. Take a risk and do something you've never done before.

A Key to Success

Have you ever noticed that the same people are blessed with success over and over? Do you know why I believe that is? It is because they have a track record of being willing to raise the roof, to stretch even though it doesn't make sense. They willingly roll up their sleeves and say, "One more time I'm going to raise the roof."

We can learn a great deal from those who have been successful in the business world. Donald Trump says, "To me, it's very simple: If you're going to be thinking anyway, you might as well think big."[2] God gave us a brain with amazing capability, but we only use about 10 percent of its capacity. He created us to think BIG.

God is the Number One Creator. He created us in His image to be creative. He wants us to use everything He has given to us, and He has given us everything we need to fulfill our purpose. Jill Elikann Barad, president of Mattel, Inc. says, "Think diversity. The idea of trying everything is important."[3] She used her creativity to launch the Barbie doll to superstardom.

> **God is looking for people who will risk *everything* He has given them to accomplish the greatness to which He has called them.**

God is looking for people who will risk *everything* He has given them to accomplish the greatness to which He has called them. He is looking for people who will take care of the little and at the same time believe God for the BIG. He is looking for people who aren't going to freak out thinking about bigger visions. He is saying, "Believe in the impossible because with Me *nothing* is impossible."

Stick with the Plan

When God gives you a plan or a vision, stick with it. Arnold Schwarzenegger came to Hollywood and decided he wanted to be an actor. A friend of mine, who is an agent, was at a meeting where Arnold Schwarzenegger announced to his manager's agents that he was going to be an action-adventure star. At that point the only movie he had been in was *Conan, the Barbarian.* It wasn't a box office blockbuster by any stretch of the imagination.

Arnold said, "I'm going to be an action-adventure star."

They said, "It isn't going to happen, besides who's going to remember Schwarzenegger?" They decided to change his name to Arnold Strong.

Then they said, "His jaw is too big. He can't talk correctly. He's muscle-bound. He would never make it as a great action-adventure star."

Arnold got mad. He had typed out a plan, and he put a copy of that plan into the hand of every single person in that room. He walked back to his seat and pounded the table with his fist. BAM! He says, "I have a plan."

> **When God gives you a plan or a vision, stick with it.**

He had a plan and it didn't include changing his name. He executed that plan and now makes over 15 million dollars a picture because he had a plan and he stuck with it.

If Arnold Schwarzenegger can have a plan to do well in movies, we ought to have a plan to do big things for God. So when you're going through a setback and getting pushed around, you've got to go back to, "I have a plan. This is what God has called me to do." And make sure it is written down so you can go back and refresh your memory over and over. Stick with the plan.

Get Rid of the "Usual"

It is time to get out of the groove. Raise the roof. Break free of old, stale habits. Leave the "usual" in the past. We are such creatures of habit. How many of us sit in the same seats at church every Sunday? You probably take the same route to work every day too.

I took my kids to a donut shop one day. As we stood in line waiting to order, the lady behind the counter greeted her regular customers. I couldn't help but notice, she could have played a recording of her conversation, "Hi, Bill, the usual? Morning, Dave, the usual? Good to see you, Bob, the usual?" She knew exactly what each of them wanted...the usual, the usual, the usual. I wanted to scream, "Lady, don't you dare give me the usual!"

I don't want the "usual" from life. Do you? I want God to surprise me. I want what has been prepared for me. It's already prepared and waiting for you to take it if you are willing to move into

> **Once you are changed you can never be exactly as you were before.**

transition. In other words, you'll have to become flexible enough to shift from one situation or state of being to another. Sometimes it is gradual, and sometimes it is abrupt like the snap of your fingers. One minute you're in a setback (snap), now you're in a comeback. One minute you're in despair (snap), now you're blessed. One minute your marriage is in trouble (snap), now it's not. This is how quickly transition, going from one state of being to another, can occur.

Transition Is a Passage

Transition always comes for the purpose of change — it does not allow us to remain the same. We are forced to move.

I view transition as a passage from one level to another. Once you pass through it, you can never go back to being the same. Once you are changed you can never be exactly as you were before. It's like the old saying, "Once you've touched the fire, you cannot live in the smoke!"

No Turning Back

Once you move into what God has prepared for you, you can't run back to normalcy. There's a "got to move" attitude drawing, stretching, pulling, kicking you. You're in transition, and you can't stay the same. Don't expect the same status quo from those who are walking in God.

> ...transition causes you to be inconvenienced....

Most of us don't want to move and shift. It may seem too much, too overwhelming, because transition causes you to be inconvenienced, disturbed, bothered and stretched. Some may even put a "do not disturb" sign on their door.

NY Times reporter, Henry Stanley, was sent to Africa to find the famous medical doctor/missionary, Dr. Livingston, and bring him back to civilization. Dr. Livingston had lost touch with the outside world and many believed he was dead. Always seeking a news scoop, Stanley was somewhat naive as to the seemingly impossible task he was undertaking.

After treking through the mountains and valleys of the unexplored interior of Africa for a year, Stanley was weary and sick with fever. He had been attacked and chased by cannibals, and his caravan had been plagued by sickness and man-eating lions with no clue as to the whereabouts or even existence of Dr. Livingston. Then a group of African tribesmen wandered into Stanley's camp and spoke of a white doctor. He went with them and found the elderly, profoundly dedicated Dr. Livingston living and working among the tribesmen, healing the sick, teaching the gospel and single-handedly exploring and mapping the vast interior of Africa.

Dr. Livingston had a vision to explore and map Africa, even perhaps finding the source of the Nile River, so that Africa would no longer be feared. He wanted to open up Africa to the world. Stanley accompanied him on some of the mapping expeditions. He was deeply impacted by Dr. Livingston's faith and purpose, unknowingly he had caught the doctor's vision. When he tried to convince Dr. Livingston to return to civilization with him, the good doctor refused, saying his work was not finished and his life was in Africa. However, he gave Stanley his maps and letters to take back to the Geographical Society in England hoping to raise interest and funds to continue the mapping.

These were not the days of faxes and e-mails. When Stanley returned to England, he was ridiculed and persecuted. The leaders of the British Geographical Society did not believe Dr. Livingston was still alive nor that the maps and letter were authentic. As Stanley was leaving the society's meeting in defeat, a letter arrived from Africa stating that Dr. Livingston had died accompanied by a letter written by Dr. Livingston in which he mentioned Henry Stanley's visit. The society reversed its vote and embraced the wishes of Dr. Livingston to continue the exploration and mapping of interior Africa.

Those who had known Henry Stanley before he went to Africa quickly discerned that he was a changed man. One friend said, "I see the spirit of Dr. Livingston in you." Stanley gave up his job with the *NY Times* and returned to Africa to fulfill Dr. Livingston's vision to open Africa to the world and dispel men's fear of this beautiful continent. Stanley had a very selfish purpose in going to Africa the first time, but God had a different purpose and plan for his return. His life was changed forever.

> **If you are willing, there is no limit to how God can use you for His purposes.**

When God has something big already set up, He looks for people who will cooperate, who don't mind being inconvenienced, disturbed and stretched while He does something huge in and through their lives. If you are willing, there is no limit to how God can use you for His purposes. It goes beyond your wildest expectations.

One day my close friend, gospel singer, Bebe Winans said to me, "Do you know who called me today? Oprah Winfrey!" He was watching her on TV when she called and said, "Bebe, this is Oprah."

He said, "Oprah who?"

She said, "Oprah Winfrey."

He said, "This ain't Oprah Winfrey. I'm watching Oprah on TV right now." He was as serious as can be.

She laughed and said, "Bebe, have you ever heard of taping a program?" She invited Bebe to be on her show. Bebe told me when they started out singing gospel music in Detroit, he never dreamed he would be talking with anyone as famous as Oprah Winfrey much less appearing on her show. God has used Bebe to touch all types of people including the president of the United States.

God Uses Ordinary People

God has no limits, and He does BIG things using ordinary people like you and me to do things that don't make sense. He believes in transition. He told Noah to build the Ark where there was no water (Genesis 6:8-22). He told Abraham to go to a place he had never been (Genesis 12:1-3). He asked an innocent young woman who had never had relations with a man to birth the Son of Man (Luke 1:26-37). Her name was Mary. He said, "I need a virgin to have My Son, and, Mary, once you move into this transition, you can never go back." Her words of faith, "Be it unto me," changed her life and the world forever.

God is looking for people who are willing to go from glory to glory no matter what the cost, because with every promise there is always a price. It may not be easy, but it may lead to someone else's destiny, someone else's breakthrough.

Make Room for the BIG

You have to make room for the BIG things in your life. Don't let your plate get so full that there isn't room for God to surprise you with something new. I know you may be thinking, "But I'm having trouble with the little things in my life, how can I ever handle anything bigger? I'm in a setback, and I can't see my way out." Put your trust in God because He cares for you. He knows when a sparrow falls from the sky. He even knows the number of hairs on your head.

As you trust God for the little things, the big things will unfold. The God idea for your life may be so big that in the natural it will overwhelm you. That is why you can't walk in the natural, you must walk in the supernatural. Ananias had to go past his natural fear and trust in the supernatural power of God to go and pray for Saul, the infamous persecutor and murderer.

Ananias' name meant "gracious." God needed somebody to really stretch out in grace because most people would have said, "Forget that guy Saul, he's killing folks." God is looking for someone who has the guts to step out.

The Guts to Step Out

God once came to David Wilkerson and said, "David, I know this will disturb you, but I need you to go to New York City and street witness to the prostitutes, pimps and drug addicts." It didn't make any sense for a white man from the suburbs to venture into inner city New York. Those people stole from him, spit on him, threatened to kill him; but he didn't give up.

He is setting you up for success whether you like it or not.

You may have seen the movie or read the book, *The Cross and the Switchblade,* about how a Puerto Rican drug addict named Nicky Cruz was set free from drugs and discipled by David Wilkerson. Nicky has preached in over fifty countries and has a beautiful wife and family because a man named David Wilkerson had the guts to be stretched and disturbed and let God bother him so Nicky could be what God called him to be.

Another one of David Wilkerson's converts is a former heroin addict by the name of Sonny Arganzoni who now has 150 churches under his direction totaling 80,000 people. This victory outreach movement was birthed because a man came to New York City and did something that didn't make sense. God had prepared a pathway for it to be accomplished, and one man stepped up to the plate in the face of danger and did it.

> **As you trust God for the little things, the big things will unfold.**

God's pathway for you is a divine setup. He is setting you up for success whether you like it or not, because it is His job to guide you, guard you and govern you. You are being set up for a transition, a shifting to another level in your faith, in your finances, in your vision.

Heavyweight boxer, George Foreman, used to be a very disturbed, angry, mean individual. One day after losing a fight, he was lying in the back room on a table, and he had a vision of Jesus, Who said, "I'm going to transform your life." George Foreman gave his life to Jesus Christ, got involved in God's process and cooperated with God's comeback plan for him which turned him into a completely different person.

The happy, smiling face you now see on TV is not the same man he was before he met Jesus. Now in his forties, George is still making millions of dollars boxing, but more importantly he is preaching in his own church and impacting the lives of disadvantaged young people from all over the country.

Stop Fishing in Shallow Water

You need to be what God has called you to be. You are the salt of the earth, the light of the world, so stand up and act like the champion you are. A lot of us have been fishing in shallow water with no results, and that is where we stop. At that point we nurse, curse and rehearse our problems with pity parties nobody else wants to attend.

It's time to throw your nets out into the deep water where the big fish hang out. It means taking some chances, taking some risks and creating a pattern of being a person who trusts God. The pathway has already been paved, and the fish are already swimming toward the nets.

Jesus borrowed a fisherman's boat to sit in while He preached to the crowds. When He finished preaching, He told the fishermen to throw their nets out into the deep. Jesus didn't say, "Throw your nets out into the deep, and you *might* get a catch." It was already a done deal. He knew the fish were there for the catching because He had paved the path. It was a certainty, and it transformed the lives of the four fishermen — Simon Peter, Andrew, James and John, who became trusted disciples. The Simon who got saved in that fishing boat was not the same Peter who died on a cross at the end of his life. He transitioned, shifted and changed from glory to glory, level to level, step by step.

People who don't throw out the net into the deep cling to their preconceived ideas of how their life should be, and their own rigid thinking locks them into mediocrity. Simon Peter broke out of the groove he was in and once he did it, he never looked back.

David approached Goliath with the same attitude. He assessed the situation and said, "This is possible. I can kill a giant the same way I killed the lion and the bear." If you get a breakthrough once, you can get it again.

A Divine Setup

The first thing God gives you to bring you into greatness, toward thinking BIG, is an invitation. He never pushes, He invites you. He may send people or circumstances into your life to stir you up, wake you up, shake you up or to help you make a decision to walk the paved pathway. It is up to you to accept the invitation.

> If you get a breakthrough once, you can get it again.

You know you're being set up when different people from different cultures and different backgrounds keep telling you the same thing, challenging you the same way. God had a purpose in opening up Africa to the world and by divine setup Henry Stanley was given an invitation to carry on what Dr. Livingston began. He chose to accept the invitation that moved his life in a new exciting direction.

Take the Easy Way

When God told Jonah to preach to the Ninevites, Jonah got set up and still didn't go (Jonah 1). The path was smooth for Jonah, but he didn't take the easy way. He had to go to Shamu

University. God loves you so much that He wants you to take the smooth path, but if He has to send a whale after you, He will do it. That is where some of you have been, stuck in a dark, cold, stinky and uncomfortable place. Did you know failure is actually more difficult and more expensive than success?

When my daughter, Chloe, wanted to get out of her crib, she would start throwing things out onto the floor. Then she would start shaking the rails, and if that didn't work even though she could barely talk, she would scream, "GET ME OUTTA HEREEEEEE!" Parents, you know how it is when you're trying to get a little one to go to sleep, and you think if you just leave her be for awhile, she'll go to sleep. Well, it really shocked us when she learned a few more words, and one night shaking the crib rails with all her might she hollered, "GET ME OUTTA HERE...I know you can hear meeeeee. Ahhhhhhhh!" At last she had found something that really worked.

Which Path Will You Choose?

Maybe you feel like Chloe did back then. In the midst of your setback, you may be screaming, "Get me out of here!" But take a moment to stop struggling against the situation you're in and ask yourself a few questions. Am I fighting to hold onto a God-given promise, or am I just fighting to get my way? Do I want out of this situation because it's unscriptural or do I want out merely because it's uncomfortable? Am I truly seeking God's will and way?

Take some time to uncover your real motivation.

You may be surprised to discover that you're bucking against God Himself. The path He has prepared for you may be far different from the way you want to go. And although it may not be the most convenient or the most comfortable, it is the best. The key is your willingness to obey Him. Obedience will help you find and begin your journey on the paved pathway.

CHAPTER 5

PURPOSE, PERSON AND PROCESS

I nside every man, woman and child is something called purpose. It's the part of us that cries out, "I've got to do something big on this planet!" Some people fulfill their purpose by helping children. Others build beautiful homes and buildings. And still others conceive of and design important new inventions. Whatever your purpose is, you can be sure, if you haven't released it, it's begging to come out.

Perhaps you don't know yet what your purpose is. If that's the case, you can be confident that God will reveal it to you as you spend time with Him. He will wake up, shake up and stir up the purpose within you. In fact, He will do whatever it takes to help you discover and fulfill what He has called you to do.

You can't do it on your own. Apart from God, you are going to be frustrated big time. It is His idea, and you must be in relationship with Him to accomplish His purpose.

Success Leaves Clues

I've met Tiger Woods and if I ever get a chance to play golf with him, I will do it in a heartbeat — not just because he has made a name for himself but because success leaves clues. If you want to get smart in the area of money, don't hang around someone who has gone bankrupt fifteen times. It works the same way with God. If you want to be all God has called you to be, you've got to spend time with Him and learn from Him.

If I could give you one clue to my success, I would say this, "I took care of the depth of my relationship with God, and He took care of the breadth of my success." He will do the same for you.

Life Isn't Perfect

Your purpose in life will never be fulfilled without setbacks, so prepare yourself for the battle and get on with it. Life isn't perfect, and that is a fact you must accept. We live in a world where the enemy is alive and well. He isn't going to allow God's purposes to be fulfilled in His people without putting up a fight. That's why we need God.

> **Life isn't perfect, and that is a fact you must accept.**

Look at all Abraham had to go through before Isaac was born (Genesis 12-21). God did the impossible by giving a 100-year-old couple a child, but it didn't happen without numerous setbacks after God spoke the promise to Abraham and Sarah. Abraham was a mighty man of God, but he was also as human and fallible as you and me. In fact it was God Who did it all, and often it was when Abraham tried to help Him out that the setbacks came. When

Abraham took his hands off and trusted God to do it, then the promise was fulfilled. It was a God-story, not an Abraham-story.

From this we know that nothing we try to do in our own might to fulfill God's purposes is going to count toward anything. It's God's plan not ours, and we must stay out of His way and trust Him to bring it to pass. Our part in the process is to trust.

Abraham is our example, our "faith" father, because he dared to trust God to perform what He said He would do (Hebrews 12:1-3,8). Against all hope Abraham believed in hope. Abraham fully believed what God said was going to happen. An important point I want to make in all this is that revelation brings conviction and conviction brings movement.

Revelation Brings Conviction

Revelation is the realization of somehting previously not known, whereas conviction is being strongly convinced to take action based upon what is known.

Just because I have a revelation that studying the Bible is good for you, doesn't mean I can get you to believe that studying the Bible is good for you. You must get that revelation yourself in order to believe it and apply it to your life. In other words, you must have a revelation from God of His purpose for your life which then brings conviction, fully believing in His promise, *before* it can be brought to pass.

> It's not about your weaknesses, your sins, your failures or setbacks. It's about what Jesus did for you at the cross.

We are too conditioned into believing that what God says can happen to others will not happen to us. We look at all of our faults, pitfalls and setbacks and say, "It's not going to happen for me." If you can get a revelation that what God did for Abraham had nothing to do with Abraham's faults or setbacks, then you can get a revelation to believe for your own promises. Get this revelation planted in your heart: Success is not about your weaknesses, your sins, your failures or setbacks. It's about what Jesus did for you at the cross. Jesus made us fit for God and set us right with God.

Fully Persuaded

Abraham was fully — not partially — persuaded that God had the power to do what He had promised. Most people are not fully persuaded God can or will do what He says, because they are so used to people breaking promises. If God says He is going to come at 6, He doesn't show up at 6:45; but a lot of our friends and business associates do. If God says there are streets of gold in heaven, we won't get up there and find streets of silver. God doesn't lie, people do.

When somebody is fully persuaded, you can see it in his eyes. You can see it in his posture, and you can hear it in his voice. When Carl Lewis ran in the Olympics, he was fully persuaded he was bringing home the gold. When Michael Jordan plays basketball, he is fully persuaded about winning the game. When Famous Amos sells cookies, he is fully persuaded they are the greatest cookies ever baked.

Conviction Brings Movement

You are going to be fully persuaded about God's purpose for your life when you get His revelation about it into your drop zone — from your head to your heart. That revelation will bring conviction and that conviction will bring movement.

Now I'm talking about real movement, power steps — steps with intent and purpose. You aren't going to be wishy-washy anymore, wavering back and forth, not knowing what is going to happen. You're going to get excited because a promise brings hope and expectation.

Giants on Every Promise

Remember what I said earlier that a promise will never be fulfilled without setbacks? It is always true because whatever God calls you to do or whenever He calls you to do it, there will be giants on top of every one of your promises. God revealed the promised land to Joshua and Caleb, but they had to climb mountains and confront giants that opposed and challenged their right to possess the promise.

In your life, they may be financial giants or relationship giants or physical giants. So, don't be surprised when they pop up, and don't let them steal your hope and expectations. This is why against all hope, against all challenges, against all mountains, against all giants, you've got to believe in hope. God is hope, and He is able to do all things. Didn't He say to Abraham and Sarah, "Is anything too hard for Me?" (Genesis 18:14)

Speeding up His Timetable

I believe God is speeding up His timetable in our lifetime, both in the natural and the supernatural. His purpose for your life is linked to His perfect timing. As He is speeding up His timetable, He is speeding up your destiny. It is critical that you receive the revelation of His purpose, believe it with conviction and take the necessary power steps to match His perfect timing if you want to become God's person in this hour. In order to do that you must follow His process.

When I was nineteen, I decided to serve the Lord with everything I had. I talked with one of my sisters about my decision, and she asked me, "What type of Christian do you want to be? What type of leader do you want to be? Do you want to train for the high school team or for the Olympics?"

I said, "What do you mean?"

She said, "I knew a girl who won a silver medal in the Olympics. She had to give it her life. At five in the morning six days a week while other people were sleeping, she was swimming. So, if you want to train for the Olympics in the realm of the Spirit, you're going to have to give it your life."

I chose to give it my life. I began to study many hours a day, to fast one day a week and to pray fervently, because I wanted to be a champion in the realm of God. It took time, perseverance and sacrifice but the prize has been worth the price.

Only One Life To Live

We only get one life on this planet, so I believe we might as well go for it with all we've got. I don't want any of us to come to the end of our days and say, "I could have been, I should have been or I would have been...."

God is raising up a championship team, and He wants you to be an integral member of that team. The question I pose to you is, "What type of player do you want to be?" Think about it carefully before you answer.

I'm sure you would agree that to have a championship team, you must first have a championship coach. Here is a good illustration. One day basketball player, Magic Johnson, was running laps with the rest of the Lakers, and his coach, Pat Riley, ran up to him and said, "Magic, you need to run faster, you're kind of loping here."

Magic said, "I'm tired."

Pat Riley said, "Everybody else is too, so keep running." Magic ran faster for awhile, and then he started loping again.

Riley came up and said, "Magic, come on. You're the captain of the team."

He smiled real big, teasing and said, "But I'm Magic."

Riley responded, "But it's my job to keep you Magic!"

A team is only as good as its coach. The Lakers had great championship players in the '80s, but it took the right coach to bring the team together and win.

#1 Coach

In order to become an effective team player, we need the right coach, and it can only be God. We have talked about the importance of trusting in the Lord, leaning on His understanding and ways, even when it doesn't make sense. If we truly want to fulfill His purposes in our lives, we must learn how to trust Him, and commit to Him no matter what comes our way.

Tennis pro, Andre Agassi, once hired a new coach and paid him over $500,000 a year. At that time Andre was not even ranked in the top five. He placed himself under the authority and the process of that coach, and you know the rest of the story. He became one of the all-time greats in tennis, winning major tournaments again and again.

Enlist in His Plan

If you want God's best in your life, you must enlist in His plan and timetable. He knows what it is going to take to get the greatest results. He sees your past, your present *and* your future. The words in this song say, "Have Thine own way, Lord, have Thine own way. Thou art the potter; I am the clay. Mold me and make me after Thy will; while I am waiting, yielded and still." Let this be your prayer.

Shaped as Seems Best

In the Bible God told Jeremiah to go watch how a potter works the clay (Jeremiah 18:1-6). While the potter was shaping the clay it was marred so the potter formed it into another shape as it seemed best to him.

Did you catch that last phrase, "As seemed best to him"? This is powerful because *you* have an idea of what your life should be like, but *God's* idea is so much better. So rather than let you create your own life, He wants to show you the great plan He has for you — shaping your life as seems best to Him. He's the potter, you're the clay.

I was walking through the supermarket one day, and I saw a little kid fighting with his mother. He wanted sweets, and she didn't think he should have them. After seeing how hyper he was, I didn't either. So Mother was pushing the cart, and he would wait until she turned her back to grab the Sugar Smacks and put them under the cart. But God has blessed mothers with sixteen eyes all over their head. Nothing really gets by them. She just simply stopped, took the Sugar Smacks out of the cart and put them back.

Was that kid mad! He never gave up. Aisle after aisle he kept trying this trick, and one of those sixteen eyes caught it every time. Finally, he went for some type of Hostess product, grabbed it and put it under the cart.

She said, "All right. Now, I've had it. I'm going to spank you." And she did it, smack on the bottom. He threw both arms up in the air, planted his hands on his hips and looked at her as though to say, "What's the big idea? Why'd you do that?"

That is exactly how we act in life sometimes. God knows what is right for us, and He brings discipline in our lives. We turn around and say, "What's the big idea? I wanted to marry that man. So what if he didn't take a bath often enough, and he chewed and spit all the time. I could have cleaned him up!" Thank the Lord He is shaping us as seems best to Him and not to us.

Live by Design

Don't fight the plan of God. Too many times we want to live by default rather than by design. There is a purpose for your life. Life without a purpose is just an experiment. If you don't live by God's purpose, you will be like a cat constantly trying to chase its tail. You'll always be looking for the end of the rainbow saying, "When I get such and such, then I'll be happy."

God has a plan for your life, and in that plan there is peace and a rhythm to life. That is one way to know if you are living according to God's will, if you have peace. Even if there are still obstacles to overcome along the way, you should have a peace and a rhythm to your life because you're in the middle of a God idea.

God's Process

I was so into this concept of the potter and the clay, that I decided to go visit a shop and watch a potter work. I discovered that each potter has a different style that makes their pots unique, but each one follows a similar, basic process. It was fascinating to see each step in the process.

First he digs the clay out of the ground. That is what God does when He takes us out of our "selfishness."

Next he soaks the clay in water to make it pliable and workable so he can mold it. That is how God works on us when we first get to know Him.

Good Coaching

Next the potter takes the clay and begins to smite it, work it. I'm convinced this is like good coaching. God brings discipline into our lives for our own good, because He loves us. He brings authority into our lives, and we don't like it. He may even use other people that we don't particularly like in the natural to teach us something we need to learn, like patience or how to control our tongue. So the next time you are having problems with someone at work, consider the possibility it may be God trying to change something in you.

So the potter begins to smite the clay, and then he takes a thin wire and begins pushing it into the clay.

I said, "Why are you doing that?"

He replied, "Because when I put the pot in the furnace, if I don't get out every air bubble, the pot will crack or explode."

Isn't that just like God prodding and looking for our imperfections? We're going to pay Him now or later. If you don't want to build character now, you're going to crack and explode a year or two down the road. God is trying to build character now, so when you get to the place of your destiny, you won't crack and explode and lose it all.

Visionary Heavyweights

We have a generation of people trying to build what I call visionary heavyweights. I'm talking about some of the motivational speakers you see on the infomercials talking about vision, vision, vision. I believe in vision and purpose within the proper context. You just can't be a visionary heavyweight and a character lightweight.

Winning friends and influencing people without having the right character is all just hype. It is out of balance. God wants you to prosper in *every* area of your life. He doesn't want you to succeed in your finances and lose your kids to drugs.

When God takes that thin wire and begins looking for imperfections, He pushes it into every area of your life. God's thin wire will challenge you about gossip, about your health and physical body, about racism and prejudice, about being a murmurer and a complainer. Why? Because our God is a long distance God. Too many of us run for the sprint, not the marathon. We think we can get away with it for the short term. But life isn't a sprint, it's a marathon.

God is saying, pace yourself and get your life in balance in *all* areas. Clean up your character now, because the old excuses won't work anymore. We can't get away with saying, "Well, this is the way I am." It is a lot easier to get rid of the air bubbles ourselves than it is to have God do it for us.

The potter puts the clay on the wheel. It was just a big lump. It's amazing how some people think they are big shots. The potter starts turning the wheel and the clay says, "Look at me. I'm really something," and the angels are saying, "That's one of the biggest lumps we've ever dealt with."

The potter starts working the clay with his hands disciplining it. "Ouch!" We don't like that, do we? But nothing good happens without discipline. You can't train for the spiritual Olympics on five-minute devotionals. Tiger Woods didn't win the Masters by hitting one golf shot a month.

God is bringing discipline to every area of your life.

God is bringing discipline to every area of your life. Some people want to own their own company, but they can't keep their car clean. They don't understand that before they can pass go and collect their $200, they must prosper where they are planted. This means paying attention to the small things such as keeping their car clean. We need to be disciplined in all things, get the picture?

Now the potter begins to shape the pot. He adds more water as needed and creates a masterpiece with his hands. God is creating you as His masterpiece molding you and smoothing out all the rough edges.

Then the potter sets the pot on a shelf to harden. In this process, you must decrease so God can increase. You're on the shelf working at Taco Bell when you know you should be running your own company. You're on the shelf in debt when you know you should be out of debt. You're on the shelf alone when you know you should be married by now, have two children and a dog named Ralph.

Meeting the Shelf Test

Shelf time is a waiting period. And waiting is a necessary part of God's process. Jesus didn't begin His ministry on earth until He was thirty years old (Luke 3:23). Moses spent forty years on the backside of the desert before he came to lead the children of Israel out of Egypt (Acts 7:23-30). The apostle Paul spent fourteen years in the wilderness getting Saul out of Paul (Galatians 1:17, 2:1) before He was fully received by the church in Jerusalem. This was all shelf time.

Here are some of the things people do from the shelf. It's lonely and you find yourself saying, "Yoo-hoo, God. Is anyone up there in the heavenlies? Doesn't anybody know I'm here?"

It's frustrating and you start murmuring and complaining saying, "I don't know why I have to stay here, I already know how to do all this. I've done it a million times. This isn't fair."

Shelf time can bring out your lower nature in the form of jealousy, and you may find yourself saying, "I don't know why

Sally got that promotion, everybody knows I have more experience than she does. Who did she brown nose?"

Sometimes we hop off the shelf and have to go back on it because we haven't learned all we needed to learn. That is a real test.

God has great plans for you, and He has you on the shelf for a reason. So how do you know when you're finished with the shelf test? When you get to the point you'll just serve Him anywhere, you'll do anything that's a God idea. Someone needs help and you say, "I can do that." It's when all the kick against the God idea has been taken out of you, and you have learned to overcome your pride. You are ready for your comeback.

> **And waiting is a necessary part of God's process.**

The potter takes the pot off the shelf. God comes and takes you off the shelf and takes you to places you could never have gotten on your own. Only God can take you where networking, motivational seminars, designer clothes and a makeover never will take you. This is when you just say, "God, surprise me!" Suddenly you find yourself owning your own franchise, as president of the company, living in a big, new house, and you say, "How did I get here?"

Prepared for Battle

The potter puts a glaze on the pot. The glaze represents God putting an increased intensity and fervor in you for the battle.

Then the potter opens up the furnace and puts the pot in to be fired.

The furnace is the new LIFE. God opens up the furnace and puts you in. This new life is a battlefield with all kinds of crazy people out there. You find out why you needed the increased intensity when He turns up the heat. The higher the call, the higher the heat goes. But He knows you are ready because He has prepared you in each step of His process.

God's Masterpiece

The most important thing to remember about being in the furnace is that you aren't in there alone. He is right there with you. You didn't make yourself. You were created by the Master. And He had a plan. He molded you, sculpted you, worked on you. You are a work of art, His workmanship, created to do the good works God prepared for you in advance before He put you in the fire of LIFE.

> Only God can take you where networking, motivational seminars, designer clothes and a makeover never will.

Ready for Use

Becoming the person God created you to be and fulfilling His purpose for your life demands this rigorous preparation process. It's not easy, but as you develop a relationship with Him through time in prayer and in His Word, this process will become a way of life. Obedience will come more easily. You'll find yourself becoming pliable in His hands — giving way to discipline more readily.

As you do, you'll begin to enjoy the results of obedience. You'll discover that success isn't dependent on your ability but on His. And as you succeed with the little things He gives you, you'll soon find yourself ruler over much. You will become a history maker and a world shaker. And you'll blaze a trail of victory not only for yourself, but for generations yet to come.

CHAPTER 6

LEAVING A LEGACY

W hen you're in the heat of the battle for your comeback, attacks may come against you on all fronts — against your physical body, your family, your finances, etc. The reason the external pressure is so great against you isn't because of you, it's because of what you represent — the generation of children behind you. It is because of the children you have and the children you will influence. The enemy isn't trying to stop just you, he is trying to kill a generation. Albert Schweitzer said, "Example is not the main thing in leading people. It's the only thing."[1] You lead by example.

A Generation of Champions

If my mother had given up as she was raising four children on her own, she would have put a "give up" spirit in all of her children. If your children see you giving up in the midst of the heat of battle, that is the kind of spirit you put inside of them. But if they see you continue to keep on fighting, you will train a generation of champions who will say, "My father didn't give up, my mother didn't give up, my brother didn't give up...and I won't either."

> **It's up to our generation to be a positive example and to encourage the next generation.**

It's up to our generation to be a positive example and to encourage the next generation. God wants our young people to be an example during their youth in areas of life where we missed it. Our children don't have to have drinking problems. They don't have to go through divorce. Our children don't have to live defeated lives. You can be the one to stir them up, shake them up and tell them there is a champion inside of them just waiting to come out. Tell them God has a plan for their lives, and they are destined to do greater things than we ever thought of doing.

Power To Encourage

It often takes the power of influence to encourage someone to greatness. In the Bible God sent a woman named Deborah to help a man named Barak fulfill his destiny (Judges 4-5). Barak's name meant lightning — swift, dynamic and powerful — but he was the complete opposite. Barak was scared of his own shadow.

Deborah came to Barak and said, "Barak, God wants you to defeat the Canaanite army."

Barak said, "I don't think so. I'm afraid." In all fairness, Barak had a reason to be afraid. The Canaanites used to cut folks' arms and legs off, and burn them alive.

Barak said, "I'm not in the mood."

Deborah said, "Don't worry; God's going to be with you."

He said, "I don't care. I'm still not in the mood."

Then Deborah said, "You're a world shaker, come on, get out there."

He said, "I don't think so. No way Jose." Then he said, "If you'll go with me, I'll go." Obviously Barak hadn't heard of male chauvinism, or else he didn't think she would be stupid enough to actually go along.

Deborah could have said, "What a loser," and walked away; but she saw Barak through God's eyes. She saw him as a history maker in her hands. That's the way we need to see our children and grandchildren. Who knows what their destiny may be. You may have a Billy Graham, or a Dr. Schweitzer living at your house.

So Deborah took this five-mile journey to go fight the Canaanite army with this guy, Barak, who's walking like a loser. She's a classy woman dressed in her Donna Karan dress and shoes. She's got her little Gucci bag over her shoulder and a donkey carrying her Louis Vitton luggage. She's walking along on this dusty donkey path trying to be classy. The first mile she breaks a heel off her shoe. By the second mile her hair has lost its bounce, and her toenail polish is chipping. She's walking along with this guy who doesn't look like he has a great destiny.

That's how some of our families used to look. Looking at them in the natural, you'd say, "Sure ain't nothing going to happen with this guy." But look how far God brought us.

At the end of this five-mile journey, Barak suddenly gets fired up, comes against the Canaanite army and whips them all. He gets those people behind him, drives his army all the way to the outer banks and becomes a champion. He even gets written up in the "Who's Who of Faith" in the eleventh chapter of Hebrews.

The question is, "What did that woman do to that man?" I believe she bombarded him with life-changing words every step of the way. Her conversation went something like this. "C'mon, you weren't called lightning for nothing. Get the lead out and move it. Act like the champion you are. Stir yourself up. Wake yourself up. Do what God called you to do. Come on, you can do it. Live up to your name. I know you've got what it takes."

Power of the Tongue

Some of you are one conversation away from greatness. Life and death are in the power of the tongue. There is a great poem that goes something like this.

If a child lives with criticism, he learns to condemn.

If a child lives with hostility, he learns to fight.

If a child lives with ridicule, he learns to be shy.

If a child lives with shame, he learns to feel guilty.

But if a child lives with tolerance, he learns to be patient.

If a child lives with encouragement, he learns to be confident.

If a child lives with praise, he learns to appreciate.

If a child lives with fairness, he learns justice.

If a child lives with approval, he learns to like himself.

If a child lives with acceptance and friendship, he learns to find love in the world.

What do your children or grandchildren live with?

One day when my son, Isaiah, was about seven years old, we were driving in the car; and he looked over at me and said, "Daddy, we have a pretty nice life, don't we? I like our life 'cause our house is kinda happy, huh?" See, that's the new generation. Our young people are going to do bigger things, creative things, if we help them up, wake them up, stir them up, shake them up and tell them they can make it.

I did some research on people who did great things at a young age. Alexander the Great conquered the world at 23. Charles Dickens wrote his *Pickwick Papers* at 24 and the classic *Oliver Twist* at 25. Francis of Assisi was 25 when he founded the Franciscan order. Billy Graham was 31 when he preached in the Los Angeles crusade in 1947 that shook the city. I believe our children will do even greater things early on.

Generation after generation of world shakers and history makers will rise up instead of the type of people we see in today's society who strike out and blame somebody else for all of their problems.

Some people strike out and others just sit out. You hear them say, "My boss laid me off. I can't believe it after I worked for this company since I was 19 years old, and I'm not even 50. I'm just going to sit it out from now on." Does any of this sound familiar?

Those who believe the promises of God, those who feast in the midst of famine, those who are determined to leave a legacy for the next generation don't strike out or sit out, because they know the power of influence. They reach out one more time. They give it all they've got and keep trying. After all if they hit that wall one more time, it may come down. They understand the law of reproduction.

The Law of Reproduction

I was walking through the streets of London when I saw a man walk out of a restaurant, and he walked just like a duck. His toes pointed out, and he took short little steps that made him appear to be waddling. His wife and kids walked out of the restaurant behind him. Those two kids looked exactly like their dad, and they walked like ducks too. That's the law of reproduction, like produces like. A lot of the mannerisms and idiosyncrasies we have, we got from our parents who in turn got them from their parents.

I have a fishing buddy from Texarkana, Texas, who twitches his neck. We were fishing for bass one time, and he kept twitching so I finally said to him, "Do you need me to pray for your neck?"

He said, "I don't have anything wrong with my neck."

I said, "But you keep moving it all the time."

He said, "My father moved his neck like this."

I said, "For real?"

He said, "Yeah, my grandfather did too."

There wasn't anything wrong with his neck, but from being around his dad, he picked up the habit of twitching his neck. Because of the law of reproduction, you learn from those with whom you spend time, either for the good or for the bad.

That is why it is so important to choose carefully those with whom you associate. There's an old saying, "One bad apple can spoil the barrel." The opposite is also true. If we hang around with people who have a "never give up" attitude, we will display that same character trait.

The apostle Paul had a fighting spirit and a "never give up" attitude. He was shipwrecked, stoned, bitten by a snake, thrown in jail with Silas in an inner dungeon with a bunch of rats all around him. He was whipped thirty-nine times and still didn't give up. You might ask, "How could he go through all that and still keep on? Where did he learn that kind of pit bull tenacity?"

> ...choose carefully those with whom you associate.

Walk the Talk

One of the places he got it was from a man named Stephen, a mighty man of God and a follower of Jesus. Witnesses were bribed to lie and falsely accuse Stephen. The crowd got so incensed, they dragged him outside the city and stoned him.

Let me tell you a little about the stoning process. An average stoning would take anywhere from seven to nine hours because they took their time using big rocks. They would start by breaking all their toes, then their feet, then their ankles and so on. It was a slow, grueling, torturous death.

Before his Damascus Road experience, Paul had been known as Saul of Tarsus — the same Saul who stood on the bank of the pit watching the crowd viciously stone Stephen and cheering them on. Even in his zealousness Saul saw Stephen endure the slow, agonizing stoning and never back off from his testimony, never cower from his God idea, never stop proclaiming the gospel. Stephen didn't get mad at God for allowing this to happen to him. Even in the face of death, Stephen kept on. Saul saw Stephen's face as he looked up toward heaven and heard him pray for mercy for those who killed him.

> **If Stephen had backed down in the midst of crisis, Saul might never have become the apostle Paul.**

Stephen walked in love even to his death, and he never gave up. In death Stephen was a powerful influence on Saul. Refusing to give up in the midst of the storm, Saul saw Stephen walk his talk.

If Stephen had backed down in the midst of crisis, Saul might never have become the apostle Paul. Without the influence of Stephen's powerful testimony, Paul might never have written Philippians 4:13 NKJV, **I can do all things through Christ who strengthens me.** He might never have written 1 Corinthians 13, the well-known love chapter many believe Paul wrote because of this experience with Stephen. Who knows how many of Paul's thirteen books of the New Testament might never have been written.

Someone's Watching

Someone is always watching and waiting for you to break through the setback you are in. Saul (Paul) watched Stephen, and Stephen watched Jesus. What will the next generation say about us? I believe there is a new generation of believers today who will not cower or back down, who will fight through for their comebacks, who will cover each other's weaknesses and lift each other up, who will stand strong in the midst of crisis and battle and keep on believing. Someone is watching you. What is he going to see when you're under pressure, when one hurricane after another is hitting your life?

It's easy to be a good example when everything is going good, but when the storm strikes how do you act? The way you act and the choices you make influence everyone around you, even those you least expect. In turn, future generations are impacted. You may not even be aware of who is watching your response.

When you bow your head to pray before a meal in a restaurant, you don't know how many others in the restaurant see you and are reminded to be thankful for what God gives to them. It may even stimulate a conversation with someone sitting nearby who needs a word of encouragement at that moment in time.

> **The way you act and the choices you make influence everyone around you, even those you least expect.**

What's Your Legacy?

What sort of legacy are you leaving for your children, your children's children, your relatives, the driver who cusses you out in the grocery store parking lot, the boss who blames you for his mistakes, the co-worker who lies to get the promotion you've been waiting for? Are you demonstrating that "never give up" attitude in the face of disappointment, loss or pain? Maybe you've gone through illness or the loss of a loved one or the pain of divorce. Whatever it is, remember the power of your influence. Someone is always watching your response. If you can't do anything else, you can leave a legacy of a "never give up" attitude. There is always hope.

Let yourself be filled with the all-powerful Spirit of God. Say out loud, "I will live a good life, regardless of setbacks! I will obtain the promises God has given me! I will live by what God says and not by what I see! That is faith. I have faith and I won't ever give up!"

One Step From Your Breakthrough

It is important to hold onto those words in the midst of setbacks. Why? Because many times a setback seems most difficult when you're only one step away from your breakthrough. That's when your enemy tries to shake everything around you. He wants to destroy you and those who are coming after you. He wants your children to see you fail. He knows that if you make it, your success will fill them with hope.

That's why you *must* hang on by speaking words of life, words of hope, words of God! Speak them and believe them. And then walk the talk, just as Stephen did in the book of Acts. And as you stick with the Word, you'll see the circumstances of your life change. And more importantly, so will everyone around you.

CHAPTER 7

GET READY FOR YOUR COMEBACK

L ife starts out with a shout. Think about it. You came out of your mother's womb shouting. Babies learn to shout when they are hungry or wet or have a tummy ache. Toddlers shout and laugh when they play together. Kids run up the steps, sling open the door and shout to Mom when they run in the house after playing outside or when they come home from school bouncing off the walls, excited about life.

Living or Going Through

We start out living life with dreams, hopes and expectations. Did you know there's a difference between living life and going through life? Living life means you have a skip in your step, a glide in your stride. You feel good, like when you were a kid and had the energy to chase down the ice cream truck, fly a kite or ride a bike. You smile just because. That's living life.

But most people just go through life. They live by default instead of by design. Their shout becomes a whisper, and their step has a hitch in it. They start feeling the sting of their set-backs as they step back once, then twice, then lose count.

Discouragement sets in. They start things but can't seem to muster up enough energy to complete them. How many New Year's resolutions have you made and never fulfilled? How many times have you said, "I'm going to lose weight?" You start out and do real good for the first couple of days. Then the new Dunkin Donuts across the street from your house has its grand opening. You decide to wait until Monday to "officially" start your diet, but Monday never comes.

Zig Ziglar says this is like biscuits that squatted to rise but got cooked in the squat. He calls such people "half-a-minders" and "gonna doers" who become "never doers."[1]

Opposition to Your Mission

> **It's not how you start, it's how you finish that's important.**

It's not how you start, it's how you finish that's important. There is always an opposition to your mission. We call them setbacks. God has already prepared your comeback so don't sit in your setback like those biscuits that got cooked in the squat. If you don't make the comeback God has for you, somebody you're sup-posed to touch won't be touched. Somebody is waiting for you on the other side of obedience to your God idea.

In a war there are casualties and injuries some of which aren't even obvious until you stop to rest. Many of us need to be healed and restored in areas where we have had setbacks.

When you're too fatigued and discouraged to finish the task before you, the Bible calls that having slack hands. When you can't shake this spirit of slackness (discouragement), it can be passed from generation to generation. Family members see this pattern repeated and begin to think, "This is just the way we live." But I believe a new generation is rising up that doesn't have to walk in slackness but rather can walk in the power of a comeback, living life instead of just going through it.

A Comeback Prepared

I keep telling you God has your comeback prepared, but let me share a famous, ageless, comeback story that demonstrates just how He does it.

A wealthy man who lived a godly life had two sons. The oldest, a college football star, graduated from college with top honors. He joined the family firm and was working hard to live up to the fine reputation established by his father and grandfather before him.

The younger son was a real party animal who didn't appreciate what he had. He begged his father to let him go to an expensive Ivy League university on the East coast. He wanted to get as far away from home as he could. On the day he left for college, he drove off in his red Porsche and never looked back.

College life was all he hoped it would be — one big party after another. He pledged the best fraternity on campus and was soon indoctrinated into beer bashes, smoking "weed" and living in the fast lane. Nothing was outside of his grasp. He started experimenting with crack and other drugs, and before he knew it, he was hooked. His habit became more and more expensive, and he needed more cash than what his monthly allowance provided.

He didn't want his father to know what he was doing so he wrote and told his father he had a chance to do an internship with an international corporation. He convinced his father to give him his share of stock from the family firm to finance getting his future career established. After all, this trip would help him climb the corporate ladder much faster. His father cashed in the stock and sent him the money with his blessings.

He lived it up with his college pals, supporting his own habit and theirs as well. Within a short time he had gone through all of his money. He sold his Porsche and pawned his jewelry. His so-called friends dropped out of sight when the money ran out. He was so strung out he couldn't hold a job even if he wanted to.

He ended up in a crack house selling crack and all kinds of drugs to support his own habit and just to exist. His body was thin and wasted. His hair and beard were long and shaggy, and his clothes were dirty and ragged. Anyone who met him on the street would not have recognized him as the bright young college student who had left home wearing Polo clothes and driving a red Porsche.

The Face of an Angel

Then one day he sold some black heroin to a beautiful teenage girl. She reminded him of a girl he had dated in high school and really cared about. The next day he was walking by a news stand and saw her picture on the front page of the newspaper. Her face, like the face of an angel, penetrated the hard shell of his heart, and he wept as he realized he had contributed to her death. Even in the wasted, confused state he was in, something brought him back into his right mind. He realized how low he had sunk. He had lost everything and now was able to appreciate what he had at home in his father's house.

He had no one to help him, but he knew he had to get out of that crack house. He said to himself, "How many of my father's employees have food and what they need to live? Here I am living in this pigpen of a crack house. I'll go back and ask my father to forgive me. I know I'm not worthy to be called his son, but maybe he will hire me to work even if it's just a minimum wage job."

His wild, indulgent life had worked for a while, but it took hitting bottom before he came into his right mind. Sometimes we are the same way. Life treats us well for awhile, but we walk a slippery path that takes us from one setback to another. The Holy Spirit finally penetrates our hard heart, and we wake up and go, "Yikes, how did I end up here?"

Nowhere to Go but Up

This young man was smart enough to realize he was in a setback, and he couldn't take any more steps back. Somehow he had to move toward his comeback. So he said, "What I've got to do is go back to my father. I know I've messed up big time, and I can't go back to the position I left. I'm no longer an heir, but I'll be satisfied with just getting in the house as a servant."

That is what the enemy tries to say to us. He says, "You've had a setback. You made a mistake. You're a failure, and you'll never be what you thought you were going to be." I'm here to tell you the enemy is a liar and always has been. No matter how far you've fallen, the promises of God for your life are still "yea and amen." God is BIG enough to change the direction of your arrow and hit the bull's-eye. If you will confess your sins, He is faithful and just to forgive you and clean you up inside and out.

> No matter how far you've fallen the promises of God for your life are still "yea and amen."

So this wayward young man made his way back home to California. As bedraggled and unsightly as he was, his father saw him coming when he was still a long way off. He ran to his son, threw his arms around him in a big bear hug and kissed him. That exuberant greeting said in unspoken words, "I still love you. I missed you. I'm so glad you're back."

God feels the same way toward us every single time we let Him down or let ourselves down. He's still our Daddy no matter how badly we behave. He's always ready to welcome us into His arms and tell us, "It's still going to be all right."

From a Shout to a Whisper

This young man was taken back by his father's response. He said, "Dad, I've been so bad. I messed up in everything I've ever done. I brought shame on you and on God. I lost everything you gave me. I smell like a pigsty, and you just don't know all I've done. I don't deserve to be treated like this." Then his voice dropped to a whisper and he said, "I'm really not worthy. I'm just here to ask for a job." His life had started out with a shout, but it had dropped to a whisper.

What did the father do? He didn't even acknowledge what his son just said. The father called to his servant and said, "Quick, bring the best suit...." In other words, the father let his son know, "That's not how we do things around this household." He had his servants bring the finest cashmere suit, put a ring on his finger and shoes on his feet. Then he ordered the feast which had already been prepared to be served.

Only By Faith

You see, even when the son was strung out on crack, living in that hell hole of a crack house, his daddy had been preparing for his comeback. He told the household servants, "You keep the ring shiny and those shoes polished. Don't you dare let any moths get into that cashmere suit because my son is coming back. By faith, he's coming back."

The servants were probably shaking their heads saying, "Humph, he doesn't even know his son lives in the worst crack house in Boston. He's hanging out with some messed up folks. And here's his poor dad preparing this beautiful suit, polishing his shoes, setting aside this gorgeous ring and keeping this banquet table full every day, all by faith."

In case any of you haven't recognized this story in its modern-day version, this is the Bible story of the prodigal son (Luke 15:11-32). It represents how God, our Father, has already prepared our comeback even while we are in the midst of our worst mess up. Did you get the message? Let it explode inside you. If He prepared your first comeback, He'll prepare your second, third, fourth and all the way to our end if that's what it takes. That's how much He loves you.

Honor Restored

The father says, "Quick, get the best robe and put it on him. Put a ring on his finger and sandals on his feet. Bring the fatted calf and kill it. Let's have a feast and celebrate. My son is home." All those things are signs of honor restored.

The father had been watching for his son from the very beginning. That's why he saw him when he was still a long way off. He recognized his son no matter how terrible he looked and embraced him even though he smelled bad. You see, he didn't look at the outward appearance. He looked inward and saw repentance, saw his son's heart change and shift. That's why he was so excited and ready to celebrate.

An Appointed Time

There is an appointed time for your comeback.

In the prodigal son's story in the Bible, the father said, "Get the fatted calf." I studied this in the Greek and it means, "Get the appointed calf. Get the calf I marked for this day." He knew the comeback was approaching, and he had already picked out the calf for the celebration. After all, a calf grows quickly so it had to be "soon." There is an appointed time for your comeback.

Your Daddy knows when you are down and out. He is already preparing your breakthroughs for this year and the next and the next.... He's already preparing the way for you. He's already preparing people to come across your pathway to bless you. They don't even know why, they are just going to want to help you.

I've had people come up to me and say, "I don't know why, but I feel led to give you this $10,000." That's my Daddy putting people in position to help me do what He's called me to do. For you it may be money or it may be the right job or the right words of encouragement or the right people to work with you. God knows exactly what you need.

His Good Pleasure

God loves to bless you and see you happy, to give you a breakthrough. Luke 12:32 NKJV says, **...for it is your Father's good pleasure to give you the kingdom.** Let's go back to the Bible version of the prodigal son story. It says the father called for the fatted calf, and it says they began to celebrate immediately. Have you ever planned a wedding or been part of planning a big event like that? It takes time, doesn't it?

One of my staff got married, and everyone was talking about it for a year in advance. I heard the bride-to-be telling everyone, "I'm going to walk down that aisle...the train of my gown is going to be flowing...and we're going to play that Bebe Winans' song...and the little girls are going to throw rose petals on the aisle...and he's going to come in from the side all handsome in his tux...." They had a year to figure it all out. So, it takes time to plan a big party and that father had been planning it for a long time in advance. That prodigal son's comeback was planned way in advance.

You may be saying, "Oh, if you knew the hell I've gotten myself in, it'll take me seven years to get myself out of this mess." That's probably true if you did it by yourself. But did you know God's "super" on your "natural" gives you the ability to do things you couldn't have done? Now I'm talking about the One with a higher power than yours, the King of kings, the Lord of lords, the Alpha and the Omega, the Beginning and the End, the Bright and Morning Star.

God is already shifting you. If you could just see in the spirit realm, you'd see the big old angels fighting for you right now. Big, bad, gladiator angels — standing there saying to your enemy, "Don't even think about it!"

I was in Nigeria, Africa, and the people around me seemed to be getting nervous so I asked, "What's the problem?"

One of the men answered, "It's the witch doctors. They say they're going to kill you."

I felt like Dorothy in the Wizard of Oz, I wanted to go back to Kansas. I'm not stupid, who wants to die in a place like that? So, I went into the meeting to preach, and these witch doctors were outside. I know they truly do kill folks. I was preaching and one of the guys on staff started screaming. I didn't know what was going on, but when I finished my message and walked out, he said to me, "I saw them, I saw them."

I said, "Saw who?"

He said, "I saw your angels."

Seven different people came up and said they saw big, bad, gladiator angels holding hands surrounding me. That's what takes place in the spirit realm on our behalf.

You are God's workmanship, and He has prepared in advance good works for you to do. Don't you think He's going to help you do them? He's not going to let one of your setbacks mess up His plans. He is all knowing and you have not blown His mind one time. He has prepared a plan, and He doesn't like to see you mess up, but He's big enough to pick you up and dust you off. So, when you're going through hell, don't stop. That's no place to camp out. Keep truckin' on through, and you'll come out on the other side of your problem or circumstance.

> **...when you're going through hell, don't stop. That's no place to camp out.**

In sports there is something called momentum that is so important. Greg Norman, playing the Masters golf tournament, was in first place when he began to lose his focus. He felt Nick Faldo behind him, saw the momentum switch, and he couldn't get it back.

In 1998 the same thing happened to Fred Couples at the Byron Nelson Golf Tournament in Dallas, Texas. He was in the lead by four or five strokes but on the final nine holes he lost his momentum. John Cook burned up the course with a 65 and took home the trophy.

Steps to a Comeback

STEP ONE: *Get rid of your "setback" mentality.* In the story of the prodigal son, the son went back to his father, dragging all the shame and disgrace along with him, prepared to beg for a menial job. This young man expected his father to react according to a setback mentality, keeping a record of all his wrongs. He would have counted himself lucky to get a halfway embrace.

He was prepared for the "look." You know what I'm talking about. You must have gotten the "look" from your parents when you were growing up. They didn't have to say a word, you just knew from the "look," you were in trouble. He was ready to hear something like: "You don't know what you did to your mother! We couldn't sleep for nights! You've wrecked our family's name and fine reputation! How could you do this after all we've done for you...?"

But the father had a "comeback/restoration" mentality from the very beginning. He fully embraced his son and brought him back into full authority as a son. Our heavenly Father extends His mercy and grace to us no matter how bad we act. He has a comeback mentality and restores us to sonship when we repent and turn back to Him. God loves to party and His "comeback" parties are better than any Super Bowl party you've ever attended!

> **Getting out of your setback is not just about survival, it's about overcoming....**

STEP TWO: *Blast through "survival" mode into a "comeback" mode.* The enemy tries to get people into a survival mode. They look at their circumstances and think, "If I can just hold on maybe I can survive." The problem is they never move beyond that point. Pulling up and out of your setback is not just about survival, it's about overcoming because you are the head and not the tail, you are above and not beneath, you're going over and not under. No weapon formed against you is going to prosper.

Sometimes God allows us to get into certain situations and places to position us to learn how to hold on by faith. So you may go through a period of holding on, but a time of stretching out must follow or you'll get cooked in the squat like those biscuits we talked about. It's time to move out of survival mode into a comeback mode.

STEP THREE: *Write down the promises God has given to you.* If you haven't written down promises that address your need, you won't be able to remember them when you are in the pressure of your setback. So write them down and read them over and over so you will remember why God put you on this planet. It will put that pit bull fight into you when circumstances look the darkest.

STEP FOUR: *Beware of dream thieves.* The enemy is a liar and a thief, and he will send people to distract you and create circumstances to drag you down. He tries to pick your pockets and steal your dreams any way he can. He doesn't like you because you have what he wanted. So if he's been attacking you lately, don't take it personally, it's because of what you represent. You may become a millionaire and support missionaries around the world. You may become the lawyer who prepares the case that throws out Roe vs. Wade. He hates what you represent.

STEP FIVE: *Expect to obtain His promises.* My father died in a car accident when I was ten years old. My mother worked in Winchell's Donut Shop, not just one shift but two. She paid her tithes and gave offerings to several ministries believing God that somehow, someway He would get her out of that situation. It was tough, but she never let her expectation level decrease.

She raised all four children in the things of God and taught us how to serve God. She stood on His promises and walked her talk when she said, "As for me and my house, we will serve the Lord." Three of us are now in full-time ministry slapping the enemy upside the head every chance we get. I thank God she never gave up. She didn't just survive, she overcame. God met her expectations.

While you're getting ready for your comeback, the circumstances may not look like what God has promised will ever come to pass. Some of you don't feel blessed right now. Some of you look at your bank account, and it doesn't look blessed. Some of you try to write a check, and the check bounces back. Some of you looked at your family last Christmas and wanted to go on daytime TV to talk about it. But I'm telling you, you're still going to be an overcomer. You're still going to obtain the promises, because all the promises of God are yes and so be it. When God says, "I will" you can bank on it, He will!

Levels of Faith

The Bible speaks of five different levels of faith: weak faith, little faith, growing faith, strong faith and great faith. Abraham did not have "weak faith." Even though his body was old and Sarah had been unable to bear children, he did not waver in his faith that God would do what He promised in giving him a son (Hebrews 11:8-12).

Jesus spoke to the disciples of their "little faith" when they awakened Him in the boat to calm the raging storm (Matthew 8:26). Paul wrote to the Thessalonians about their "growing faith" (2 Thessalonians 1:3). Abraham had "strong faith" and was fully persuaded God was able to do what He promised (Romans 4:21). Jesus spoke of the centurion soldier's "great faith" when he asked Jesus to heal his servant (Matthew 8:5-13).

The faith you use to hold on is the same faith you're going to use to stretch out and do everything God has called you to accomplish. It's just a different level of faith. Anyone who works out in a fitness center knows that building muscles requires persistently stretching

> **The faith you use to hold on is the same faith you're going to use to...do everything God has called you to do.**

and pushing to higher levels. That's exactly how you build your faith muscles.

I believe we have all been doing faith exercises without even knowing about it. Some of us started back in the '80s with weak faith then we moved to little faith. In the early '90s we started exercising our faith muscles and our faith started growing. In the mid '90s we were stretching for things that required strong faith. Now in the late '90s we realize it is going to take "great faith" to move into the next millennium.

I remember when it was hard for me to believe God for a thousand dollars to go overseas, then two thousand, then ten thousand. Now I have faith for half a million when it's needed to do something great for God.

When I started exercising my faith muscles, seeing myself preaching to ten thousand, then twenty, then thirty, and on up into the hundreds of thousands, I saw myself preaching all over the world, and everything I was seeing began to happen. At eighteen I couldn't get into Oral Roberts University. At twenty-five I was teaching there.

Do you catch the drift of what I am saying? I'm not sharing this with you to brag on what Tim Storey has done. I want you to realize this never could have happened with a "survival" or "just hang on" mentality. Holding on doesn't scare the enemy, it's when you stretch out that he gets nervous. People who stretch out have influence and impact — life-changing and life-saving impact.

Comeback Champions

Vince Lombardi was one of the greatest football coaches of all time winning 74 percent of his games. He was a man who inspired and motivated his players to victory. When he took over the Green Bay Packers in 1959 the team had only won one of their twelve games in the previous season. In his first year as coach, the Packers won seven games. The next year they played in the NFL championship game and lost to the Philadelphia Eagles. The Packers then won the NFL championships in 1961, 1962 and 1965 as well as the Super Bowl in 1967 and 1968.[2]

Coach Lombardi took a team of losers and turned them into champions by teaching them how to stretch out and reach higher. His teaching methods were commitment, sacrifice and mental toughness. He expected dedication, intensity and sacrifice from his players. He believed that if you treat people with respect, treat them like winners, they will be winners. He blasted the Packers out of a survival mode into a comeback mode.

Vince Lombardi said, "Once a man has made a commitment to a way of life, he puts the greatest strength in the world behind him. It's something we call heart power. Once a man has made this commitment, nothing will stop him short of success."[3]

Poised for Your Comeback

Just like Vince Lombardi, you must be willing to put out the effort it takes to be a champion. No matter how much you've lost or how far down you've gone, you must leave the past behind and move toward the future. You've got to swing into comeback mode.

Start now by making a commitment to your own success. Next write down God's promises and keep them before you. Believe them. Use those written promises to stay focused on where you're going. So that when opposition comes, you know that you are already on the road to comeback.

CHAPTER 8

HOLDING ON TO YOUR PROMISES

B efore your God-appointed ascension (your comeback) takes place, the enemy's attempted assassination (a setback) will try to prevent it. You may be one step from your breakthrough when all hell breaks loose. When I was a little kid chasing the ice cream truck, flying my kite and beating up my neighbors, I never knew life could have so many strange turns. Everything would be going great. Then all of a sudden "bam," along came a turn of events that didn't just rock the boat, it deployed a depth charge.

My father died when I was ten, a tough age for a boy to lose his dad. Three years later a call came that my sister had been in a terrible car accident. We went to Modesto, California, to pray for her. She was in a coma for eight days and then died. That's what I mean by a depth charge. Everybody in the family was having a hard time. Some were messing up big time, but I watched my mother as she kept believing, kept trusting, kept holding on to the promises of God.

A "Yes, I Can" Spirit

According to *Webster's Dictionary*, a promise is a vow that provides a basis or reason for expectation of success, improvement or excellence.[1] It is a reason for hope. When God gives you a promise, it pumps you up and you say, "Yes! I can do it." You may have to flex your faith muscles to obtain that promise, but once you get the "Yes, I can" spirit down in your heart, you're on the home stretch to your comeback.

I can remember in sixth grade we had to do the President's Physical Fitness Test. One of the guys in class we called "little Ricky," wasn't little at all. He had a hard time doing even one pull-up. But we loved Ricky because he was funny. So when the teacher wasn't looking we would help him up, one...two...three. We'd say, "Hey, look at little Ricky, ohhh that boy can do some pull-ups." We'd help him out so he did okay on his test.

But as he struggled with each pull-up, he started saying, "I'm gonna...I'm gonna...I'm gonna do...I'm gonna do some of them things...I'm gonna lose some weight." Sure enough by eighth grade Ricky was doing pull-ups, swoosh, swoosh, swoosh. He caught the "Yes, I can" spirit and held on to his promise.

When I was in Bible college some friends asked me if I wanted to go see a man by the name of Paul [David] Yongii Cho.

I said, "Is he the one who wrote the book, *The Fourth Dimension?*"

They said, "Yeah."

I said, "Let's go."

We hopped into my Honda Civic and drove four hours to hear this man who had had tuberculosis as a teenager, was healed and believed God for a great church in Seoul, Korea.

He stood at the podium and in his broken English said, "You must believe the Lord; you must believe the Lord; you must visualize what the Lord can do."

Preaching on great faith, he said, "There are measures of faith. You can grow your faith. I started with faith for a church of one thousand, then two thousand, then ten thousand. Now I have faith for a half a million."

He did everything he said. He had a "Yes, I can" spirit. He understood the promises of God and never stopped believing until he obtained each promise.

When we got in the car to go home, my friends said, "We drove four hours and he was boring." One of them said, "I couldn't even understand him." But I caught the man's spirit. There was no more "just hanging on" for little Timmy Storey, hoping I wouldn't do something wrong. I started flexing my faith muscles and stretching out to obtain the promises.

God's Four P's

When God gives you a **p**romise, He'll give you a **p**lan, He'll show you His **p**urpose, and then He'll make **p**rovision. He's taken me around the world fulfilling His purpose in my life, and He always makes a way.

> When God gives you a promise, He'll give you a plan, He'll show you His purpose, and then He'll make provision.

I can't tell you what it feels like to preach hope in the inner cities and see guys drop their Colt 45's, get down on their knees and let Jesus change their lives. It's exciting. When you know the hell you came from and then bring hope to someone else, you can't help but shout.

A God Idea

When God gives you a promise, it is a God idea. There's a difference between a good idea and a God idea. Good ideas come from the mind of man. God ideas come from the mind of God. Good ideas *may* come to pass. God ideas *will* come to pass. There's no doubt about it.

> There's a difference between a good idea and a God idea. Good ideas come from the mind of man. God ideas come from the mind of God.

Here's an example of a good idea and a God idea that demonstrates how God's idea often has a greater purpose than we can compehend at the moment. On one of his missionary journeys, the apostle Paul wanted to go preach in Asia, but God said, "That's a good idea, but it's not My idea." (Acts 16:6-40.)

As Paul and Silas continued on their way, every city they tried to stop in, God said, "No. That's a good idea, but not My idea."

Then one night Paul had a vision of a man calling them to come to Macedonia. He knew it was a God idea. So, they traveled to Philippi, the foremost city in Macedonia. After being there for several days, Paul met a woman by the name of Lydia, a wealthy merchant in the import/export business. She was the first person to open her heart to the message Paul was teaching down by the river. She and her household all got baptized, and she invited Paul and Silas to come stay in her home. She started having meetings in her home to tell others about the Jesus Who changed her life.

As Paul and Silas walked about the city, a servant girl who was demon possessed kept harassing them. Finally, Paul decided enough was enough and cast the demon out of the girl. He was feeling good. Life was great and he was singing the song, "I Got a Feeling Everything's Gonna be All Right." But life was about to take an unexpected turn.

The servant girl's masters were angry because Paul hit them in their pocketbook. They were using this servant girl as a fortune-teller to earn lots of money. These dudes were so mad they dragged Paul and Silas before a judge and incited the crowd against them. The judge ordered Paul and Silas to be stripped and beaten. That wasn't a cool situation.

Now who sent Paul to Philippi? It wasn't his mother-in-law, it was God. That's right. In the middle of a God idea, all hell can still come against you. Life is not perfect just because you are following God's plan and purpose. In fact, that's when the battle gets more intense.

> Life is not perfect just because you are following God's plan and purpose. In fact, that's when the battle gets more intense.

Things went from bad to worse with Paul and Silas. Not only were they beaten until their backs were raw meat, the next thing they know they were chained to a wall in the inner prison with big rats running everywhere. Their feet were in stocks stretching them to the point of breaking their pelvic bones. This wasn't a pretty sight.

Singing His Praises

But watch Paul's response. He didn't cuss God out or fax the other disciples and say, "It's just not worth it, this business of serving God." No, he and Silas responded by praying and singing praise songs to God, and the other prisoners were listening. Let's get real. Most of us wouldn't react that way. More than likely we'd be saying, "God, I must have missed You on this one. Get me outta heeere!"

You can really tell what somebody is all about when they are pressed. What is inside of them will come out. Paul and Silas were pressed, and they sang praise songs.

I'll be honest. When I first started out serving God, that's not how I responded. When I was in Bible college, I studied the Bible and prayed a lot, but I'd go through seasons of really messing up. I'd be doing really great and then just get stupid. Can you identify with what I'm saying? I'd be studying, praying and believing God for big things, and then nobody would invite me to preach. I was called to be a preacher and no one would invite me.

I remember one night I was so mad, I decided I was going to quit the ministry. I was driving around in my Honda Civic listening to Teddy Pendergrass, "Turn off the lights," I decided, "I'm not going to be a preacher, I'm going to be a Teddy Pendergrass." You know how little kids are when something goes wrong, they throw a tantrum? We need to get out of those tantrum days.

Paul and Silas were pressed and they just kept praising. Can you just hear the beat? They were rappin' for Jesus, "It's still gonna work. It's still gonna work." And don't forget the other prisoners were listening. Somebody is always watching who needs your testimony.

"Suddenly" Is God's Style

When midnight came, *suddenly* an earthquake shook the whole prison. God always shows up. He will never leave you when you're in the midst of a God idea. He does things *suddenly.* That's His style.

So the earthquake hit and all the doors in the prison opened and everyone's chains fell off. This is important. Paul and Silas were the ones who praised God, but their response in the midst of their trial didn't just loose them, it loosed everybody around them.

Who Flicked His Bic

> Paul and Silas were the ones who praised God, but their response in the midst of their trial didn't just loose them, it loosed everybody around them.

You know the old saying, "One bad apple spoils the whole barrel"? It's the truth, just like one positive person can change the whole atmosphere in a group. I've seen it happen when I used to do weekly Bible studies with the Oakland Raiders.

It's Monday morning, and everybody's sitting there beat up with ice packs strapped to every imaginable part of their bodies. In walks Rocket Ishmael. He's the kind of guy that everywhere he goes it's like somebody just "flicked his Bic." So the guys are beat up, feeling bad, and here comes Rocket. "Hey, man, what's happenin'? Man, you're lookin' good. Hey, man, I'm tellin' you...." His personality energizes the whole group.

One guy being optimistic in the midst of being pressed can loose the chains off the whole group. If we get loosed, we can loose our family. It only takes one to get out of the pit and then get the whole family out. Noah built the ark and saved his whole family (Genesis 9:1-19). Joseph got loose, then he got his brothers loose (Genesis 41-47). Rahab, the prostitute, got loose and got her whole family loose (Joshua 2).

I like what the great preacher E. V. Hill in Los Angeles says about this episode with Paul and Silas in the prison. He says, "I believe the angels were enjoying the song and stomping their feet to the beat and it caused an earthquake."

All storms die out eventually.

Suddenly chains come off. It can happen if you'll keep on keeping on and ride out the storm. All storms die out eventually. God will not take you through things you cannot handle because He's given you His power. Just keep believing in His promises.

The Best Is Yet to Come

The best part of Paul's story is yet to come. The jailer woke up, saw all the prison doors open and assumed the prisoners had all fled. He drew his sword and was going to kill himself rather than face death at the hands of his superiors. In Roman times if a prisoner escaped, the jailer was punished and killed by methods that weren't pretty. Now watch this. Even though it doesn't seem like it at the time, a lot of the trash we go through has a reason behind it. The chains come off and here comes the reason for the prison experience.

The jailer was about to kill himself when Paul called out, "Time out, man. Don't get bloody here." Don't you know that jailer was nearly scared stiff? He called for a light, ran in and fell down trembling before Paul and Silas.

The jailer brought them out of their cell and asked, "What must I do to be saved?"

Paul said, "Believe in the Lord Jesus, and you will be saved — you and your household." The jailer and his entire household were saved and baptized that very night.

It's About the Future

The entire prison experience was a divine setup. God will lead you into places that are divine setups. It may not feel good, but God sees the whole picture. It's not just about the present, it's about the future. Paul later wrote a letter to the believers in Philippi which became the book of Philippians, the greatest motivational book in the Bible. He would never have written that letter

> The entire prison experience was a divine setup. There are places God has you that are divine setups. It may not feel good, but God sees the whole picture.

to Philippi if he had not gone to Philippi in the first place. It was God's idea.

Scholars believe the jailer was the first pastor of the Philippian church. He went to Lydia's Bible study, was taught by Luke, the physician, and then given the church. Sometimes you find the greatest gems after the most difficult expeditions.

One day I was watching a University of Southern California football game. The USC defensive back intercepted a pass and ran forty yards toward his end zone. He had a towel hanging from his pants with something written on it. He ran all the way for a touchdown, and the announcer said, "There's something written on his towel." The other announcer read it to the crowd, "Philippians 4:13, **I can do all things through Christ who strengthens me**" (NKJV). The crowd went wild.

Imagine if Paul hadn't been obedient to a God idea, if he'd given up and hadn't gone through the beating, the chains, the rats, and still praised God. There wouldn't have been a young black man in the Coliseum two thousand years later running all the way for a touchdown with Philippians 4:13 printed on his towel as a testimony to thousands of people.

Through it all, out of the depths of his spirit Paul was saying, "God is able. He can still do it. It's going to be all right." When you keep the right attitude in the midst of the mess, you're saying, "I believe God above my circumstances. I believe God above my own stupidity. I believe God above everything I am. Even if I'm a knucklehead sometimes, God isn't a knucklehead. I still believe God." Let me tell you something about life. You're going to let yourself down but God is still able.

In the midst of a mess, in the times of greatest pain, in those desert experiences we gain our greatest revelations of God. David wrote his greatest psalms in the midst of his deepest pain. When Paul became a Christian the other disciples didn't want to hang out with him. They rejected him because they didn't trust him. So where did he go? He went to Arabia, that's the desert, the wilderness.

> When you can't go forward, backward or sideways to get out of where you are; you have to go up and that's where you bump into God.

When people reject you, don't understand you, stab you and twist the knife, leave you or forsake you; the point comes where you don't know who to go to, what to do or where to go. When you can't go forward, backward or sideways to get out of where you are; you have to go up and that's where you bump into God. It's in those where-can-I-go-but-God experiences that God gets you all to Himself and you hear Him most clearly. He wants you one-on-one because He loves you and wants to talk with you face-to-face.

One-on-One

My father and mother had five children, but I loved it when my dad got with me one-on-one. He'd take me to Little League practice, look me in the eye and say, "Timmy, you're going to be someone special. Timmy, you're a champion." I loved those one-on-one times with my dad.

Some of us get so busy making things happen, earning a degree, dating, getting married, buying a house, losing weight, playing with the dog, climbing the corporate ladder, serving God, we don't take time *for* God. You're sliding and gliding through life, but God's been trying to get some one-on-one time with you. After all, He created you and put you on this planet to have a relationship with Him. So He will shift things around to get you to Himself if that's what it takes.

Firsthand Revelation

So Paul was in the Arabian desert and he got a revelation from Jesus Himself (Galatians 1:12). He didn't get it second-hand from Peter or the rest of the boys. He got it directly from the top. I believe you can live a good life based on second-hand revelation, but to live a God life you must have firsthand revelation. That's how you really get to know Him.

When you get a firsthand revelation, something changes inside of you. It brings conviction. That's why a salesman must personally get a revelation that his product works and is the best there is in order to be successful in convincing others to buy it. He must be a product of the product. Paul was a product of the Product — Jesus.

> **When you get a firsthand revelation, something changes inside of you.**

Another thing about a revelation is that it takes time. That's why you have to spend some time in the desert to let it soak inside of you, to get marinated in God. Paul spent years in the desert soaking in the revelation he received before he went to Jerusalem and was accepted by the other disciples.

Let me give you an illustration of the importance of a revelation. I went to see Michael Jordan play baseball in Birmingham, Alabama. That's right, I said baseball! Optimist that I am, I was wishing for the best. It was raining and hardly anybody was in the stands. Jordan was in right field looking bored. Come on, six foot six in a baseball uniform wearing his hat too high, he just didn't look smooth like when he's on the court.

Bam! A guy hit a ball to right field. Jordan got caught in the lights and with the rain coming down, the ball hit the ground. He picked it up; it was all soggy; and he was thinking, "Why am I out here?" He didn't have a revelation that he was good in baseball. The spirit of Willie Mays had not hit him.

But in basketball Michael Jordan dares you to guard him. It's like he's saying, "Bring me one person, bring me two people, bring me three. You bring me two, I'll go by you. You bring me three, I'll shoot over you. I'll stick my tongue out. I won't bite my tongue, and I'll still slam dunk." Michael Jordan has a revelation about basketball. You see it in his eyes and in his stature. You see it in everything about him.

In the '80s Carl Lewis knew he could not be beaten in track. When he ran, he knew he was going to win. He was so confident, people thought he was cocky, but he had a revelation that he was Carl Lewis. He worked hard and trained hard. He was famous for the way he bowed his chest way out going over the finish line. He was so set on winning, he didn't even look for anybody else. He just threw out his chest, flew across the finish line and went looking for the gold. That's why when he crossed the finish line in one of his Olympic races, he didn't even realize Ben Jonson from Canada had flown right past him. He came off the track and said, "Where's the gold?" Somebody said, "What gold, Ben Jonson beat you."

Carl was blown away and insisted something was wrong. A lot of people said, "He's a crybaby. Look at the way he's complaining." But, sure enough, Ben Jonson tested positive for steroids. He was juiced up and that made him go faster. What he did was not really humanly possible. Carl Lewis knew inside himself that he was Carl Lewis.

That is how you must live when you hold onto God's promises. You're not going to cower down, back down, give up or cry the blues listening to old Hank Williams' songs. You're going to get a revelation that God did not bring you this far to leave you, and you aren't going to die in the midst of your storm.

Life is not perfect, and you will not cross the finish line perfect. You'll have some setbacks that may mess you up. I don't care how far off target you've gone, God can put you back on the right track because of what Jesus did at the cross.

> **I don't care how far off target you've gone, God can put you back on the right track....**

Paul said to Timothy, "I was the 'worst of the worst' but look what God did with me. If I can do it, you can do it!" I remember the pain and loneliness I felt when my dad died and again when my sister died but I made it through and so can you.

By His Grace

In the midst of pain God's amazing grace just lifts you up over the impossible circumstances. A lady stood up in a black church and gave her testimony.

She said, "I've been going through some trials. But I don't feel no ways tired. I've come too far from where I started from. Nobody told me this road would be easy, and I don't believe He brought me this far to leave me."

A young man 17 years of age sat at the Hammond B3 organ and began to sing that testimony in song. *We may not be where we want to be, but thank God we're not where we used to be.*

Stick With His Promises

I believe God has spoken to all of us and told us certain things to do. You may not realize it was God, but you are His creation and God has a plan and a purpose for your life. That's why you aren't going to be a failure. God gets more glory out of you being a success than out of you being a failure. If you've had more failures than successes up to this point in your life, then now is the time to change the pattern of your life and stretch for your comeback. One way to do that is to stick with His promises.

> **...God has a plan and a purpose for your life. That's why you aren't going to...fail.**

If you don't know what His promises are, ask God to tell you what He thinks about you, what He's going to do in you and how you're going to do it. Get that one-on-one revelation directly from Him. Then believe God really is BIG enough to bring you back to a place of stature and significance. He will even take you beyond where you ever thought you could go, because that's what God does. When He restores, He doesn't just take you back where you were, He takes you one step higher.

Even in the midst of what other people would call failure, don't give up. If He lifted you out of a setback once, He'll lift you out again. The Bible says a righteous man falls down seven times but he will rise up again (Proverbs 24:16). When you hold on to your promises, even if you have a setback, you won't step back because you know in your heart, God has already prepared your comeback.

CHAPTER 9

SLAYING THE GIANTS

D id you know three giants are sitting on top of every one of your promises? They sit there big and bold saying, "I dare you to knock me off!" Try as they might most people never knock off all three of these giants. They may hit one or maybe two but the third one eludes them, and they never possess their promise. These three giants have been stealing promises from God's people for thousands of years, and they are just as powerful today as they were in the days of Moses.

When Moses led the people of Israel out of Egypt, God promised them a new land. It was a God idea. They wandered in the desert for a time but when they came to Canaan, God said, "This is it. This is your promised land. Go check it out." (Numbers 13.) It was never a question of whether or not they could possess the land, it was just a matter of surveying what was there and what they needed to do to possess it. God wanted them to see how bountiful it was and to know how they needed to prepare for living in it.

Moses chose 12 men to explore Canaan and he said, "Go walk through the country. See what the land is like. Is it good or bad? How is the soil? Is it fertile or poor? Are there trees or not? Do your best to bring back some of the fruit. Find out what kind of people live in it. How many are there? What kind of towns do they live in? Are they unwalled or fortified?"

The 12 men did what Moses told them to do and returned carrying huge bunches of grapes to show the fruit of the land to others in the camp.

They confirmed what God had promised was true. The land flowed with milk and honey. But they also reported that the cities were very large and heavily fortified and the people living in the land were powerful. In fact, they were the descendants of Anak who were giants and old enemies of Israel including the Amalekites, the Hittites, the Jebusites, the Amorites and the "Pepsi-lites." (Just wanted to see if you're paying attention!)

Expect Opposition

Every time you have a God idea, obedience is required, and there will always be opposition to your mission. You cannot avoid it, but God will always be your strength to overcome it. Expect the opposition. Don't be surprised by it and do whatever is necessary to be prepared for it. Many people who have a God idea never get through the opposition, and they never fulfill their purpose or destiny. You're going to have to face some old enemies, and you're going to have to do battle.

> **Expect the opposition. Don't be surprised by it and do whatever is necessary to be prepared for it.**

The Israelites weren't expecting any opposition to their promise. They thought they would just march in and have a great life. Let me tell you something. God gives you the sight, the right and the might to do great things, but you have to develop the fight!

Develop the Fight!

The 12 men Moses chose to go spy out the promised land were the best Israel had to offer. Ten came back with a negative report. Only Caleb and Joshua had a good report. In Numbers 13:30 NIV Caleb said, **We should go up and take possession of the land, for we can certainly do it.** It's the "spirit of Caleb" you need to accomplish your God idea and possess your land, that "just-do-it" attitude.

Be careful with whom you choose to associate. Don't spend time with negative people. It rubs off. They say, "You can't sell houses in this area, there's a recession," or "We should all move because a giant earthquake is going to hit and California is going to fall into the ocean."

Doesn't that sound just like the report of the 10 Israelite spies who said in Numbers 13:32 NIV, **The land we explored devours those living in it. All the people we saw there are of great size.** Have you ever had someone say to you, "Don't even try going there. Don't even try to be a success. You'll never make it. The obstacles are too big, they'll devour you"?

Isn't it amazing that when you face opposition to a God idea, the enemy says, "This is the worst problem you've ever faced. You can't do this." Don't buy into his lie. No matter how impossible the circumstances *appear* to be, God prepares a way.

A Grasshopper Mentality

The 10 Israelite spies bought into this sort of lie and saw nothing but defeat because they had a grasshopper mentality, as it reads in Numbers 13:33 NIV: **We seemed like grasshoppers in our own eyes, and we looked the same to them.**

It was true, the people who lived there were giants with a nasty reputation. But the spies weren't grasshoppers in the giants' eyes because the enemy knew the God the Israelites served. They didn't look like grasshoppers in God's eyes. They only looked like grasshoppers in their own eyes. It was their own perception. It's like the saying, "What you see is what you get!" If you see yourself as a loser, that's what you will be.

...see yourself as a champion.

Do you remember the cowardly lion in the movie, *The Wizard of Oz?* Everyone else knew he was a lion, but he didn't have a clue he was a lion. He was afraid because he didn't know who he was. Don't be like the cowardly lion. God sees you as a champion. The enemy knows you are a champion. You've got to see yourself as a champion. It's never going to happen unless you learn to slay the three giants that sit on top of your promises.

Giant #1 — Fear

The first giant is exactly what defeated the cowardly lion, fear. Fear is an emotion of alarm and agitation caused by the expectation or realization of danger. Have you ever heard fear defined as "False Evidence Appearing Real?" If God calls you to do something great, fear always attacks you.

Giant #2 — Doubt

The second giant is doubt. Doubt means to be undecided or skeptical about something. It's a lack of conviction. It's being double minded. One minute you're up; the next minute you're down. You say, "Well, I'm pretty sure it will work, but I'm not too sure." Or, "I think tithing works, but I'm not too sure."

Giant #3 — Unbelief

The third giant is unbelief which means "not to believe." To believe means to place trust in or confidence in someone or something. So when you have unbelief, you're saying, "God's Word is not good enough." You're not trusting or putting confidence in God, the great I AM. If not God, then who? There are only two choices left; yourself or the enemy. Think about it.

Do you remember the U.S. Olympic basketball team, the Dream Team? They had Michael Jordan, Magic Johnson, Larry Bird, Charles Barkley. They went into the Olympics knowing they could whip everybody. And they did! Moses sent his Dream Team into the promised land but they came back with fear, doubt and unbelief saying, "Whew, the giants are bigger than God." That's what they said by their actions as well.

> ...your giants are not bigger than God.

God Is Bigger

I'm here to tell you, your giants are not bigger than God. Alcoholism, depression, divorce, all the things that have attacked your family in the past are not bigger than God. It's not about believing in yourself or having confidence in yourself, it's about believing in the ONE Who sent you, the ONE Who commissioned you, the ONE Who told you to possess the land. It's not just faith in you; it's faith in Him, that He's able to do what He said He would do.

Three-way Remedy

I want to give you a three-way remedy to kick these giants off your promise every time.

1. You must have proper knowledge.

2. You must have proper relationship.

3. You must have proper experience.

Knowledge brings things into the right perspective. When you are fighting a giant you have to be knowledgeable about the situation in order to bring it into perspective to eliminate the fear, doubt and unbelief. In the military it is said that you must know the enemy in order to prepare a winning battle strategy. This is true in spiritual battles as well.

> **Giants will shout back. That's why you have to become knowledgeable of the Word of God and how it works.**

Here's an example. Do you remember when we feared Russia? When I was in school, the Cold War was still raging and we feared the big, bad bear known as Russia. We had air raid drills and had to go sit in the school hallway in case Russia dropped a bomb. As if that really would have helped!

All we ever saw of Russia on TV was the big, bad Russian army marching through Moscow with their tanks and rockets being displayed. When communism fell and we finally got into Russia, we saw all kinds of problems, including a devastating alcoholic rate, a high abortion rate, a lack of food and living essentials, etc. When we obtained proper knowledge about life in Russia, we saw things with a different perspective. The Bible says in Hosea 4:6, **My people are destroyed for lack of knowledge.**

Some of the things we fear really aren't that scary. This story is a perfect example. A minister friend of mine asked me to go with him for a week to Calgary in Alberta, Canada, to spend some time praying and seeking the Lord. I said, "Okay, that sounds great."

Then he said, "I'm going to take my bow and arrow, and I want to buy you one."

I said, "I'm not really into bows and arrows. I'm from the city."

He said, "Come on, it's fun, great recreation." So he bought me a bow and some arrows and paid for lessons on how to shoot at a target.

I said, "Fine, I'll go shoot at a target."

This guy was a bit of a comedian and two days before the trip he said, "Now listen. We're going bear hunting with bows and arrows."

I said, "Well, forget you. I'm not going bear hunting with any bow and arrow! I'm afraid of bears. I don't even like to go to the zoo."

He said, "It's too late. The trip is already paid for. Tim, you need some adventure in your life. You're always caught up in helping everybody else; this is going to be good for you."

What could I do? I said, "Okay, I'll go and shoot targets. Maybe one time I'll go out there with you, but hunting bears is not for me. I want to go fishing or something else."

Dressed to Kill

We arrived in Canada and I discovered he had found out my size and bought me a complete camouflage outfit. Then he told me I had to paint my face. Can you picture this? I'm a city boy from Los Angeles, and the guides knew I was no great hunter. They were laughing and teasing about how afraid I was of bears. All night around the campfire, they were telling stories about bear attacks and about how bears can run faster than horses and climb trees. It was bear night.

Money Talks

I was so freaked out I couldn't sleep. Every time I heard the tent move, I'd start praying, "Oh, Jesus, that's got to be a bear...." You had to be there to appreciate it all. The next morning we were up at the crack of dawn which was fine with me since I hadn't slept a wink anyway.

We were each assigned to a hunting guide. Mine was the youngest in the group, 22 years old, chewing tobacco and spitting a lot. I was not excited about this excursion at all. I decided money talks so I said to my guide, "I'll pay you extra money. This is just between you and me. Don't take me around any bears. Do you understand? I don't want to see any bears."

So he said, "Okay. I'll take you to an area where we haven't seen any bears for weeks. Just do what I say 'cause they're already teasing you."

If you've never been on a bear hunt let me enlighten you as to how this works. They take you out in the woods, and you have to climb up on this thing called a tree stand. Then they put out bait about 20 yards away and cover it with branches. They throw out some donuts with syrup to try to lure the bear in.

My trusted guide took me to my tree stand and said, "Don't worry about anything. You ain't gonna see no bear."

I was feeling good as I climbed up on this tree stand. I had on my boots, my camouflage, my green hat. My face was all painted up real good. Then my guide told me to rub this scent on so the bear couldn't smell me. It was made with fox urine and came in a tube. Well, that's where I drew the line. No way, Jose. This city slicker wasn't about to put it on.

I was all settled down in the tree, and all of a sudden I heard, "Blaaaa, Koahhhh...." Here comes Gentle Ben in the flesh. I'm not kidding. This bear was tearing through the woods crushing everything in his path. I've never been so scared in my life.

Come on. I had only been shooting a bow and arrow for two days. I don't like heights. I don't like the wilderness. I don't like bears. I was shaking so hard my teeth were chattering. I was thinking about what those guys said, "They'll climb trees, rip your face off, chase you down if you try to run." My life was passing before my eyes. I was finished for sure.

Just Kill Me Quick!

The bear came closer. He was sniffing the air. I was thinking, *Why didn't I put on that fox urine?* He was sniffing me. He was seeing me. I was trying to hide behind a little branch of that tree and praying like I've never prayed before. It's true, I was hiding.

He struck a bear pose. I was so scared I honestly thought, "I'm going to jump out of this tree and just let him kill me quick." Don't laugh at me. Put yourself in that situation. You're in a tree staring down the throat of a big bear with only a bow and arrow, no gun, no knife. Honestly, it was torment.

This bear and I went at it for awhile. He was smart. That's how he got so big because no one had gotten him yet. He started looking for the donuts, making sure his body was shielded from where I am. He was watching me the whole time. He got himself a glazed donut, staring at me as he licked his chops. He gobbled down his donut and took off crashing through the woods down toward the river.

I breathed a sigh of relief, "Thank You, God." But he was still hungry and back he came. This time he was really messing with me, growling and snarling. This was not a good sign. He was mad. He was agitated. He was thinking something bad.

Don't forget the three giants and the three ways to kick them out. I was experiencing the worst fear I've ever known but suddenly knowledge I had learned from a video surfaced in my mind. I love to study and the man who gave me the bow and arrow lessons had said, "You're such a bad shot, I'm going to give you this video on how to shoot the bow and arrows, how to shoot a bear, where to shoot a bear and how to know what is happening in the mind of a bear." I watched that video over and over again. I started to become knowledgeable.

My mind was so flooded with the scary stories those guys had fed to me around the campfire, the fear had pushed the knowledge I had right out of my mind. I knew he was coming up to get me.

But suddenly I got mad. I was shaking like a leaf. You're supposed to strap yourself in and then shoot. I was so scared I couldn't even stand up. There was a big branch in front of me, and I knew if I was going to get a clear shot, I was going to have to lean on that branch. I was nervous but I remembered what the man said in the video. I could see the diagram he used. He said, "When you hunt a bear, don't hit it in the foot, you'll just aggravate him. Don't hit it in the head or the buttocks, you'll just make him mad. Try your best to maneuver yourself to get a good shot at the vitals. Hit it right in the chest."

This bear had been working me over for 35-40 minutes. I felt like dying. I couldn't take it any longer. He gave me one last growl, and I said, "It's either him or me." My mind clicked into knowledge and that bear made one bad mistake. He stretched too far, and I was able to let one arrow go and oh well! Now, do I believe in killing animals for sport? Not necessarily. Do I believe in being alive? Yes. Will I ever do it again? No. Am I glad I am not there right now? Yes. But I'm still alive.

Fear Cripples

What can we learn from this true story? Fear can cripple your mind. The stories about the bear made my mind go crazy. Even after the bear was hit and started running off into the woods, I thought, "He's going to bring his family back. I'm not out of the woods yet."

When the guide found me, I wish I could have jumped down and strutted my stuff saying, "Man, I killed myself a bear." But I was still up in the tree shaking because I thought the bear would bring his family back. His cousins were going to be mad and beat me up like a big bear gang. Is that a ghetto mentality or what?

How do we knock off fear or doubt or unbelief? With proper knowledge. Because knowledge about a situation brings it into proper perspective to eliminate fear, doubt and unbelief. And with proper relationships because as you build your relationship with God, you won't be fearful anymore. Your Daddy didn't bring you this far to leave you. He won't drop you in the water to let you drown. He doesn't lift you up to let you down. When you truly know Him, you trust Him to pull you through. Proper relationship brings proper faith.

The last remedy for kicking out the giants is proper experiences. Look at the giants you have kicked off in the past. When David faced Goliath, he already had proper experiences in killing a lion and a bear with his bare hands (1 Samuel 17:31-37). He wasn't afraid of Goliath. All of his brothers and the rest of the army were tormented with fear, doubt and unbelief. Fear will paralyze you if you let it. When I looked at that bear, I was paralyzed until I tapped into the knowledge I had.

David said, "I can do it the same way I did it before. I killed the lion. I killed the bear. I can take down Goliath the same way." God will give you proper experiences to build your faith so you can slay the giants in your life.

Giants Shout Back

Fear is one of the most powerful weapons the enemy uses to cripple people. I want to make one more important point. I was with a pastor who was building a large 4,500-seat church. They were halfway into the building project but the money wasn't coming in. He said to me, "Every time I drive by that church, it's like the building tries to yell back at me and say, 'I will never be built.' I finally realized it was the voice of the enemy."

Your giants will shout back at you. You may hear, "You'll never lose weight. You'll never be healed. Your kids are going to stay messed up. You'll never be married."

Giants will shout back. That's why you have to become knowledgeable of the Word of God and how it works. God is bigger than any giant. Believe not in yourself but in the ONE Who is able. Get closer to God. Relationships are built over time so make it a priority to spend time daily reading the Bible, praying and singing songs of praise and worship. He will keep you in perfect peace if you keep your mind on Him (Isaiah 26:3). Cast your cares upon Him because He cares for you (1 Peter 5:7). God rewards those who diligently seek Him (Hebrews 11:6). Seek Him with all your heart.

Lastly, stand on past experiences and victories no matter how small they may seem in your eyes. If you can't think of any positive past experiences, then look in the Bible and gain strength from those men and women you read about — David,

Rahab, Ruth, Peter, Paul or any others. Don't back down. You're a professional giant killer.

CHAPTER 10

DESPERATE FAITH

D esperate circumstances trigger desperate faith. When you run out of rope, it's time to grab onto faith. It's time to get mad at the enemy and take up the fight. It's time to do something different to change your life from failure into success. Sometimes we have to get to the end of ourselves before God can mold us into the vessel of honor He desires us to be.

Seeds of Encouragement

When I was a little kid, I struggled in school. The fact that my teacher said I was the biggest class clown she had seen in a long time didn't improve my reading skills. My mother kept telling me, "You can make it!"

About that same time, I had a Little League coach named Ron Trejo. My dad had died, and I needed a man in my life to believe in me. Coach Trejo said, "Tim, you've got championship qualities, but you have a bad attitude and a bad temper. You've got to stop cussing everybody out."

I had an anger inside of me, but Coach kept on believing in me. He stayed with me even after I left his team. When I was eleven, twelve, thirteen, fourteen, fifteen, Coach Trejo kept coming by the house to make sure little Timmy Storey was okay. He touched my life, taught me discipline and helped change me into what I am today in God.

Fifteen years later, I was able to sow seeds of encouragement back into Coach Trejo's life. I looked out my window and saw him walking across the street toward my office. He was facing a desperate situation. It was my turn to say to Coach Trejo, "You can still make it! Don't take a step back. You can get up from that situation and go forward. Get up one more time. Come on, it's inside of you." I'm thankful to God that Coach Trejo didn't step back, he came back, and has coached four more teams to national titles.

A Different Kind of Touch

We can learn a great deal from a woman in the Bible who demonstrated desperate faith. She had been bleeding for more than 12 years and had exhausted her strength and finances seeking help from the medical community. No one could help her. She was considered unclean and untouchable according to the laws of her culture.

She was sick and tired of being sick and tired. She heard about Jesus and determined that if she could just touch the hem of His garment she would be healed. She wasn't going to strike out and blame anyone else. She wasn't going to sit it out and never live a normal life. In her desperation, she reached out with desperate faith.

The crowds were so overwhelming it looked as though she would never be able to move close enough to touch Jesus. She didn't let that stop her. She did what she had to do. She dropped to her hands and knees and started crawling through the dust and dirt and donkey dung. All she could see were sandals and dirty feet, but she didn't give up. She kept saying, "I will live life again. I will be a wife to my husband again. I will be healed." Imagine how she felt when she saw the hem of Jesus' garment, and reached out and touched it.

> **She dropped to her hands and knees and started crawling through the dust and dirt and donkey dung.**

It was a crazy crowd. The Bible says Jesus was thronged by the crowd. That means there wasn't room to move. People were everywhere. She didn't touch Him on His skin, she just touched His cloak but He felt it.

He said, "Hey, who touched Me?" His disciples thought He had lost it because there were so many people touching Him.

He said, "It's a different kind of touch." It was a touch of desperation and faith. Jesus turned and said, "Woman, your faith has made you whole."

This woman did four things from which we can learn:

1. She *"heard" about Jesus*. We need to have ears to hear.
2. She *said in her heart*, "If I can just get to Him, I will be healed." We must make a heart decision and not let go of it.
3. She *put action to what she felt she had to do*. We must take action and step out in faith.
4. She *got out of her situation, out of her setback*. We will never make it to our comeback until we leave our setback behind.

No More Wet Sheets

> Jesus
> turned
> and said,
> "Woman,
> your faith
> has made
> you whole."

A little seven-year-old boy reached a point of desperation and decided he was going to get to Tim Storey. I was speaking at a church and was in a room after the meeting.

He told the ushers, "I must talk to Tim Storey, right now."

They said, "You know, he's tired. He's been praying for people...."

He wouldn't give up and said, "No, I must talk to Tim Storey, right now!"

One of the ushers came into the room and told me there was a little boy who needed to see me. Kids are so cool.

This little guy came in and said, "Hey, heart-to-heart talk between me and you."

I said, "Okay," and took him aside.

He said, "You're gonna heal me, 'cause I got a problem."

I said, "Okay."

He leaned real close and whispered, "Just between me and you, I wet the bed."

I said, "You know everybody's done it."

He said, "But it messes me up, man. 'Cause I can't go to Boy Scouts or to Little League sleepovers. So, go ahead and heal me."

Desperation is a great motivator. He was sick and tired of wetting his bed. He decided in his heart to get to me no matter what. I prayed for him and sent him on his way.

Sometime later I was preaching at another church in the same city. Walking through the crowd, I felt somebody yanking on my jacket. I looked around and saw a little guy standing there.

He said, "Hey, I'm the guy you prayed for," and named his church.

I see so many people so I didn't recognize him, but I said, "Oh, man, that's right."

He said, "Remember what my problem was?"

And I said, "Well, help me out."

With a slam dunk motion he smiled and said, "No more wet sheets."

Turn Stumbling Blocks Into Stepping-Stones

You can use your stumbling blocks as stepping-stones. When you go through hard times, use them for fuel. Say, "I'm not going to live like this. I'm not going to be down or depressed. If I have to crawl to Jesus, I'll do it. I'll get up one more time. If I have to study more or break up with a knuckleheaded boyfriend, I'll do it. I'll do whatever it takes to change my life to get better results." God responds to desperate faith. He's a miracle-working God.

> **When you go through hard times, use them for fuel.**

It Only Takes One To Get Out of the Pit

My favorite story of all time is about a childhood friend named Mikey. Every neighborhood has a Mikey. He was nine and I was eight. He came to me and said, "Timmy," that's what they called me back then. He said, "We're all gonna play hide and seek in the sewers underneath the rich neighborhoods."

I said, "That doesn't sound too cool."

He said, "No, it's great fun. We get flashlights and it's real dark, just right for hide and seek."

I said, "You all go ahead." I was a clean freak.

They took off and came back all muddy, smelling like a sewer, but they had the time of their lives. I agreed to go along to play this hide and seek game with Mikey and seven other guys about the same age.

When you're that age you don't read the L.A. *Times* or watch the weather channel to see what the weather is going to be. Besides that, when you're down in the sewer you don't know when it starts to rain. So we were down in the sewer having a blast playing hide and seek. In California it doesn't just rain, it pours. It started raining and suddenly the water level started rising in the sewer lines.

In case you've never had the pleasure of being in a sewer, let me explain. There are different sized drums but the best hiding places were in the smaller ones. We had little guys stuck in these smaller drums everywhere when the water started to hit them. We thought we were going to drown for sure because the drums would fill up completely.

We all started running toward the larger drums, sloshing through the water, getting downright desperate. Everyone was screaming and dropping their big K-Mart flashlights. It was complete chaos, but in the midst of this I said, "Hold it. I gotta find Mikey."

Mikey loved those sewers and knew them like the back of his hand. He was the sewer king, that was his "anointing." All these kids were crying and waiting for me to go find Mikey.

Mikey came and I said, "Okay, Mikey, lead us out of here." I lined up all the kids, one behind the other, with Mikey in front. Each one held onto the belt of the one in front of him. These kids were just looking for someone to lead them out of the storm. They were looking for someone who had answers.

Mikey started running with everything he had. Kids were holding on for dear life. They went left. The water was coming up fast. They went right. Mikey knew exactly where he was going.

Notice that not one kid stopped and said, "Are you sure you know which way you're going?" When you're dying, you're just looking for somebody who looks like they know the way out. So, Mikey led us through the maze of the sewers.

Another important tidbit about sewers is that you've got to know which manhole to pop open or you'll get your head cut off. Mikey went to the right manhole. The water was coming up higher and higher. We were really sloshing. He popped off the cover, and we all scrambled up the ladder to the street. We collapsed on the pavement trying to catch our breath. We were all safe because Mikey was the sewer king. In that place of desperation we looked for someone who knew the way.

I believe our families are looking for somebody who knows the right way. They've got pressure, conflict and setbacks. Life is just flooding them. Many have been in the sewer of life and things are coming up higher and higher. These are perilous times. That's why you must rise up and say, "ENOUGH IS ENOUGH." Somebody has to be the Mikey of the family.

You've got to be sick and tired of seeing anyone in your family messed up. I believe the setbacks you have been through have given you a new strength. When you reach the point of desperation, like the woman with the issue of blood, you're going to rise up and say, "I'm not living in the pit of fear, unbelief and doubt any longer. I'm getting out of this situation. I don't care who puts me down or who doesn't understand me. I'm going to get help and that help is Jesus."

It only takes one to get out of the pit and then pull the other members of the family out too. If God can wake you up, shake you up and help you become a world shaker and a history maker, you can help to breed a new generation of family members who will live in victory instead of defeat. Get up one more time and go meet your miracle. It's time to raise up a new generation of champions!

CHAPTER 11

RAISE THE ROOF ON YOUR EXPECTATIONS

I t's time to take the ceiling off and raise the roof on your expectations. Nothing is impossible for God, and He has proved it over and over and over. He is in the miracle-working business. If God can make the heavens and the earth, He can find you a godly, loving spouse. If God can part the Red Sea, He can provide you with a new job. If God can pave the streets of heaven with solid gold, He can show you how to get out of debt. Nothing is impossible for Him.

Certainly Means Certainly

It's time to start thinking bigger and reaching higher. It's not good enough just to get through the struggles and setbacks. It's not good enough to barely get by each month. It's not good enough to have three good days out of seven.

> **It's time to start thinking bigger and reaching higher.**

The word *certainly* is mentioned in the Bible more than 1,200 times. When God says *certainly* to you, He means it's fixed; it's determined; it's settled; it's done. In street slang that means, "Sure enough; I ain't teasing; or I ain't fronting." Did you catch that? God will supply all of your needs. He is the same yesterday, today and forever. God is speaking certainly's into us. His *certainly's* are God ideas.

> ...you will never move on something in which you do not truly believe.

The enemy has tried to fight you in every way to stop you from getting God's certainly's into your spirit. It's one thing to get a certainly in your mind. It's another to get it deep down into your spirit. When you get it in your spirit, it will cause you to do great things because you will never move on something in which you do not truly believe. Say to yourself right now, "I'm going to get a certainly in my spirit!"

God spoke a certainly to Abraham in the Bible when He told this ninety-year-old man he was going to have a son. Abraham semi-believed as he was dialoging with God. Sarah, his wife, heard what God was saying and laughed because it seemed so ridiculous.

The plan God has for you is so big, it will seem ridiculous to your mindset. Abraham and Sarah's miracle was already in motion, and when they let that *certainly,* the promise of a son, drop deep down in their spirits, God gave them the desire of their hearts.

God will do the same for you. I'm with people every day all over the world, common folks, who are believing God for big things, and they're happening. I get to hear testimonies in such places as Singapore, Sweden and Trinidad. God is no respecter of persons or of geographic areas. His principles work for all people, in every culture.

It Had To Be God!

Although we had never met personally, Lee Iacocca invited me to his home for dinner one evening. As I drove up in front of his mansion, immediately his staff was serving me, parking my vehicle, showing me into the house, introducing me to Mr. Iacocca.

> The plan God has for you is so big, it's going to seem ridiculous to your mind-set.

I was in awe that Lee Iacocca, Mr. Chrysler, who earned $30 million a year and at one time had the number one best-selling autobiography in America, would want to meet with me much less invite me to a private dinner at his home.

After dinner we sat in the living room, just the two of us, and he said, "Mr. Storey, tell me the secret of your success. I've watched your videos; it's amazing what has taken place."

I said, "It has to be God because I come from four generations of alcoholics. We were the poorest of the poor BUT GOD...."

That dinner and conversation was a God idea that opened the door for me to spend numerous one-on-one sessions with Mr. Iacocca talking with him about the principles of God's kingdom. It had to be God.

You're going to live an "it had to be God" life as well. You're going to look at your family following after the ways of God and say, "It had to be God." You're going to look at your restored marriage and say, "It had to be God." You're going to look at your new house and say, "It had to be God."

The places God is going to take you may seem ridiculous in your mind, but when it's a God idea anything is possible. It's time to lift the ceiling and let God be God. You've been living with 4-foot ceilings when God is ready to raise the roof right out of sight.

> **God is no respecter of persons or of geographic areas. His principles work for all people, in every culture.**

The Bible says in Psalm 78 that we must tell the generations about the miracle-working power of God or they will become stubborn and rebellious. Isn't that what we are seeing in America today? Young people are stubborn and rebellious because they have lost hope in their tomorrows. We've got to show our children by our actions that God is a big God. We have to take our faith to a higher level not just for our own sake but for the sake of the next generation. I don't care what the circumstances look like, against all hope believe in hope. Don't stagger at the *certainly's*, the promises of God. Wear hope on your face.

Jump the Facts

Some of you may be saying, "But Tim, you don't understand some of the facts about my life. I have this problem with my weight and I've tried everything." Well, guess what. I believe God is going to give us Christians supernatural ways to lose weight. We're going to start eating right, walking and aerobicizing and acting right. If Oprah can do it, we can too.

When you need the energy to do what God has called you to do, your body has to keep up with your vision. God's going to help you jump the facts that you are 20, 50 or 100 pounds over-weight. God's going to help you jump the fact that your finances are in the pit.

Pure Beauty

Aimee Mullins is a beautiful, ener-getic, twenty-two-year-old athlete and fashion model. She has been jumping the facts all of her life and raising her expectations to do the impossible time after time after time. Why is that? Because Aimee is a double amputee who says, "The truth is, I'm sort of lucky to have this body, because it forced me to find my strength and beauty within. So, if I don't turn my legs into a big thing, others don't either. And if I let them see who I am inside as well as outside, hopefully they like me for me."[1]

> We have to take our faith to a higher level not just for our own sake but for the sake of the next generation.

Aimee was born with a deformity which could have kept her bound to a wheelchair. The fibula, one of the major weight-bearing bones in the lower leg, was missing in both of her legs. With great courage her parents made a decision when she was only one year old to amputate her legs so she could be fitted with prostheses. Aimee literally took her disabilities in stride and was walking by the time she was two. She now has four dif-ferent pairs of legs: one for everyday use, one for swimming, a special graphite pair for running and a special cosmetic pair for looks.

Aimee says, "I decided at an early age to transform any set-backs into strengths and tackle them head-on."[2] That's exactly what she has done. In her childhood there was nothing her brothers did that she wouldn't try and master. She swam, played soccer, skied and had her own paper route which she delivered on her bicycle each morning. In college she competed on a Division 1 track team with able-bodied athletes. Today she is an avid runner and holds two world records in the Paralympics, (athletes with disabilities), despite the fact that a double-amputee's body requires three times as much energy to exercise as a regular body and 40 percent more oxygen.[3]

She never tries to hide who she is or the fact that she is an amputee. Wearing shorts or miniskirts doesn't bother her at all. She uses every opportunity to help others learn to be comfortable with her disabilities. She has co-founded HOPE (Helping Other People Excel), a nonprofit organization that provides training for disabled athletes and has plans to help amputees get artificial limbs. She says, "Let me be the one who changes fear into understanding and makes people comfortable with amputees. Who knows? Maybe little by little, I can change the world."[4]

Aimee Mullins' entrance into the fashion modeling world was a goal far beyond showing off her pretty face. She has set her expectations to do runway shows and photo spreads in order to redefine what "beautiful" really means. She explains it this way, "As a model I can confront society's emphasis on physical perfection and say, 'Hey, look at me. You think I'm hot, but guess what? I have artificial legs!' There is no ideal body. Mine is very imperfect, and I can't change that — but I can still be attractive. Confidence is the sexiest thing a woman can have. It's much sexier than any body part."[5]

Aimee doesn't deny the fact that she is an amputee, she has jumped the facts with a positive, unbeatable attitude. She faces setbacks daily, but she has learned the secret of turning them into strengths by facing them squarely and pressing forward instead of stepping back. She is sowing seeds of greatness into others' lives and gains great joy and satisfaction from it. Aimee is a history maker and a world shaker who is making a difference helping others raise the roof on their expectations.

Giants on Your Promises

You'll hear me say many times in this book, "You will always find giants on your promises." It's time to square up and face the facts. Become knowledgeable and understand the facts, but most important be honest with yourself. There is power in honesty. It is a fact the giants are there, but God is going to give you breakthroughs and make a way when there seems to be no way to hurdle the facts. He'll start by giving you the faith to jump one fact, and then you'll have faith to jump another and another. You'll find yourself saying, "It had to be God."

How do you think Daniel felt when he was staring in the face of a dozen hungry lions that had been eating Christians for breakfast, lunch and dinner? He had to jump the facts and believe God could shut the mouths of hungry lions so he could fulfill God's destiny in his life. That story is probably one of the most famous in the Bible and has been told over and over for thousands of years to give people hope in desperate situations. God is the same God today as He was in the days of Daniel.

I believe God has been doing some big things, but we've been so busy trying to work through our struggles that we've missed the big things.

Shift Your Dish

I was at a friend's house to watch a football game. He lives out in the country and had just bought a new satellite dish. He was excited and couldn't wait to show it to me.

He said, "Tim, watch this new satellite dish, wherever I shift the dish, that's what I pick up. I can watch games on the East coast, in the Midwest or anywhere."

It struck me. That is what we need to do. Wherever you shift your dish, that is what you will pick up. You can shift your dish toward "All things are miserable. Life is hard. I don't know if I'm going to make it." Or you can shift your dish to the "All Things Are Possible" Miracle Network. When you shift your dish toward God, you get a miracle mindset.

One of my friends, who plays for the San Francisco 49er's, was with Bill McCartney when McCartney was getting the vision for Promise Keepers. They would go out walking and McCartney would say, "I may be crazy but I see stadiums filled with men." He wasn't off, it was a God idea.

We've seen stadiums all over America filled with 50,000 men holding hands, crying, hugging and sharing each other's needs. Men are stepping into their rightful place as leaders in their homes and families are being restored. Now it's spreading around the world. I've been in Sweden, Norway and England and heard men talking about Promise Keepers. It takes a miracle mindset to do something like this.

If God is speaking to you about something that seems ridiculous or crazy, don't walk the other way. Shift your dish and jump the facts. You've got a miracle in the making. Start acting and living like the champion you are. You've got the best Coach and He's a big God.

God's Rearranging the Furniture

Sometimes in order to position you to fulfill your destiny, God has to rearrange your life. When God called me into the healing ministry, I had never seen anybody healed. He said, "You're going to travel all around the world." At that time I hadn't traveled eighty miles away from home.

I needed to raise the roof on my expectations. God had to rearrange my surroundings and my friendships. It's like when you move into a new house, you have to find a new way to arrange the furniture. God had to bring people into my life who had a *miracle mentality. Today* I still purposely get around people who will stretch me.

> **Sometimes in order to position you to fulfill your destiny, God has to rearrange your life.**

God is stretching you right now as you read this book. Just getting out of debt isn't going to be enough. Now you're going to lay up money for an inheritance for your children's children. No longer will blind eyes seeing be a hard case. No! You're going to start seeing as Jesus sees. He's going to stretch you. You're going to learn to stand on His certainly's, walk on His certainly's, run on His certainly's and soar on His certainly's as you raise the roof on your expectations.

CHAPTER 12

IT'S STILL GOING TO BE ALL RIGHT

D on't you love the feeling of excitement and anticipation when a new opportunity opens up in your life? That was the way Simon (Peter) and his brother, Andrew, felt when Jesus walked by their fishing boat one day and said, "Come and follow Me, and I will make you fishers of men." They threw down their fishing nets and picked up that promise. They were filled with hope and expectation. This was a new adventure, "fishing for men." They had enough zeal and energy to take on the world.

I love to be around children because they have so much energy. It doesn't take a lot to get them excited about something new. When my daughter, Chloe, was six, I took her to buy some new Nikes. She picked out exactly what she wanted, a pair just like Ashley's, her best friend. It was cute to watch her look at them in the mirror as she walked back and forth. After we paid for them, she insisted she had to wear them out of the store. She had to walk in front of the mirror again on the way out. As she walked along the mall, she kept looking down at them. We stopped for ice cream and she kept looking at them and again when she climbed into the car. She couldn't keep her eyes off those new Nikes. She was excited when she got home and ran into the house to show her brother, and she couldn't wait to show them to Ashley.

How long do you think those new shoes held Chloe's attention? It wasn't long before the newness wore off, scuff marks appeared, and they were just another pair of shoes. We've all discovered it's one thing to start something new, and it's another thing to be in the middle of it when the glory begins to fade. A family vacation is glorious the first few days but by the end of the week you can't wait to get everybody back home.

A Dose of Reality

After three and a half years, Simon (Peter) and Andrew were seasoned veterans following Jesus. Great things were happening. They were preaching, praying, healing the sick, casting out demons. They were living life, feeling pretty confident about themselves, maybe even a little cocky. Just about that time along came a big dose of reality. Jesus saw it coming and warned Simon (Peter) saying,

> **Simon, stay on your toes. Satan has tried his best to separate all of you from me, like chaff from wheat. Simon, I've prayed for you in particular that you not give in or give out. When you have come through the time of testing, turn to your companions and give them a fresh start.**

> **Luke 22:31** THE MESSAGE

Peter responded like little Arnold often did on the TV show, "Different Strokes," saying, "Whatchyou talkin' 'bout!" Or, in more modern terms he was saying, "NOT!" Peter was rugged, strong-willed, passionate, expressive and overconfident. He never did anything halfway. He was feeling good. He was living large. So when Jesus said Satan was going to come after him, Peter said, "It's not going to happen to me. Maybe it'll happen to 'doubting' Thomas or to that crybaby, John. It's obvious he has emotional problems. I saw Judas stealing from the moneybag. It may happen to him. But it's NOT going to happen to me." Peter's pride got in the way of his heeding the warning. Jesus said, **I'm sorry to have to tell you this, Peter, but before the rooster crows you will have three times denied that you know me** (Luke 22:33 THE MESSAGE).

Later that evening when the soldiers came to arrest Jesus, it was Peter who struck out and cut off the right ear of the servant of the chief priest. Jesus knew that no matter how Peter reacted, in the end Peter was going to be all right. Jesus reached out and put the man's ear back on. Don't you wonder what the soldiers thought when they saw that miracle or what the conversations were later that night in the servants' quarters at the chief priest's house?

When the soldiers took Jesus away, Peter followed at a distance. You don't backslide overnight. You don't gain weight overnight. It takes time. Peter has been hit and hit and hit by life. He's always in the middle of things or out in front, but now he's at a distance. Before that night was over Peter had denied three times that he knew his beloved Friend and Master, Jesus. When the rooster crowed, Peter was vehemently cussing and denying he was part of Jesus' group. Jesus turned at that moment and looked directly at Peter, as if to say, "I know you failed, but it's still going to be all right." At that moment Peter realized what he had done, and he went outside and wept bitterly.

Peter went from rugged, strong-willed, passionate, expressive, overconfident and feeling good to feeling ashamed, confused, guilty, shocked and caught in the grip of hopelessness. That's what can happen in life. You can find yourself in a situation you never thought you could be in. It may be a job that leaves you unfulfilled, a marriage that is a battleground, a body you don't like, a life you don't feel is worth living. The enemy hits you and you take a step back. He hits you again and you step back again and again. When you find yourself in a setback, don't step back, because God has already prepared your comeback, just as He had for Peter.

> **When you find yourself in a setback, don't step back, because God has already prepared your comeback,...**

Comeback on His Mind

Let me prove to you that Jesus had Peter's comeback on the forefront of His mind. On the third day after Jesus was crucified and put in the tomb, Mary Magdalene and two other women went to His tomb to anoint His body with oils and spices. Reaching the tomb, they found the large stone had been rolled away from the door, and an angel said, **"Don't be alarmed," he said. "You are looking for Jesus the Nazarene, who was crucified. He has risen! He is not here. See the place where they laid him. But go, tell his disciples and Peter..."** (Mark 16:6,7 NIV).

This is the only time in Scripture we see Jesus singling out someone from the team of disciples. In a Swedish Bible translation it says, "Go tell the disciples, *especially* Peter." When Jesus went to the cross, He had Peter on His mind. When He went to the grave, He had Peter on His mind, and when He rose again, He wanted to be sure Peter knew everything was all right. He wanted to remove that look of failure from Peter's face.

The face tells everything about a person. It is a mirror of your feelings or emotions. You can put makeup on your face. You can have layers burned off with acid or a laser. You can have a facelift or have your lips injected. But what you are feeling will still show on your face. If you're guilty, it's on your face. If you're sinning, it's on your face. If you're full of shame, it's on your face. But if you look at hope, you're going to look hopeful.

Promise of a Happy Ending

Jesus took Peter's setback and comeback personally, and He takes yours personally too. Jesus must have been saying, "I've got to get that look off My friend, Peter's face, because last time I saw him he looked confused, shocked and torn up!" "Torn up" means "he didn't look too good!" Jesus was saying, "It's not over. It's still going to be all right. This story is going to have a happy ending." Don't you like that?

I was taking my children to a Disney movie; and my daughter said, "I'm not going to even go in unless this one has a happy ending. The last one you took me to about the gorillas didn't have a happy ending. This one better have a happy ending." See, that's how we are in life. We want to know something is going to have a happy ending. Am I going to meet my goals? Am I ever going to fulfill my God ideas? Will my marriage break out of this rut? Will I lose this weight? Will we ever pay off these debts?

Jesus is the Author and the Finisher of our faith (Hebrews 12:2), and it's still going to be all right. You're going to have a happy ending. You may be saying, "Right now I don't feel too good." It doesn't matter, because Jesus is personally going to help you with your comeback.

So Peter is feeling down, confused, messed up, ashamed. He's looking through the want ads in the *Jerusalem Times*: "Wanted: One Cussing Fisherman." One of the disciples from the inner city stops by and says, "Peter, what's up, man?" Peter says, "I'm just looking through the *Times*. You know, my life's all messed up since I denied Him. I guess I need to find a new job."

Just then one of the other disciples comes running in and says, "Man, you're not going to believe it! I just got a message. You're not going to believe it! They saw Him."

Peter says, "Saw who?"

The excited disciple answers, "They saw Jesus. He's risen just like He said He would. He's alive. He's all holy and glowing. They said He sent a message to tell all of us, and He especially mentioned you, Peter."

Peter was in a state of setback. When you're in a state of setback, you're caught in the grip of hopelessness. You wonder how you're going to ever get out. It's like being stuck in cement. Peter is there! But a promise brings hope into his spirit. Your hope will see you through as well. That's why the enemy doesn't want you to have hope. He tries to bring discouragement and despair to keep you in the cement.

Could've, Should've, Would've

Everyone of us has swallowed a dose of reality and experienced the pain of a setback. We all have a could've, should've, would've story. If only I'd stayed in college, I could've been a doctor by now. I should've listened to my parents and made better choices for friends, then I would've been leaving for college next month instead of facing jail time for car theft. If a dream dies, there is a grieving process, but you don't have to stay in the grieving posture. Did you know God

> **If a dream dies, there is a grieving process, but you don't have to stay in the grieving posture.**

gives life to dead things? It says so in Romans 4:17 NIV **...the God who gives life to the dead and calls things that are not as though they were.**

A Promise Gives Hope

Lazarus was a fourth-day miracle. He was part of Jesus' inner circle of friends, and when he became deathly sick while Jesus was in another city having a healing meeting, his sisters, Mary and Martha, sent for Jesus to come immediately. The messenger came and said, "Hey, Jesus. Lazarus is sick." Jesus spoke these important words. He said, "This sickness will not end in death." It was a promise. When God speaks, He does not lie. He watches over His Word to perform it. So when Jesus said the sickness would not end in death, everyone believed Him.

His promise produced hope. Hope is the light at the end of the tunnel. Hope lifts your spirit when you feel discouraged. Hope helps you keep going when you feel like quitting!

One day when I was about eight years old, my daddy came home and said, "We're going to Disneyland on Thursday." I was so excited about going to see Mickey Mouse, I dug out my old Mickey Mouse ears from three years earlier. I had to use bobby pins to keep them on top of my big Afro. It was only Tuesday but I wore those ears and barely slept for two nights waiting for Thursday morning to arrive. My daddy had made a promise, and my hope and expectations were sky high.

When Jesus said Lazarus' sickness would not end in death, the messenger headed back to Mary and Martha singing, "I got a feeling everything's gonna be all right."

Jesus took His time and stayed to finish up His healing meetings. Let's bring this story into present day. The disciples are concerned and one of them says, "Hey, did Mary or Martha e-mail you or beep you on your pager about how Lazarus is doing?"

Jesus says, "Everything's all right. Our friend Lazarus is sleeping. I'm going to wake him up." The disciples are thinking, "Great. He must be doing better." They didn't get it. Then Jesus told them plainly, "Lazarus is dead."

It looked like Jesus' promise had died. Lazarus had been dead and in the tomb for four days by the time Jesus and the disciples arrived there. Everyone was grieving and crying. But Jesus had a reason for waiting. The Jews believed that the spirit of a dead person hovered over the grave for three days and in that three days by some miracle, he might come back. But after three days it was completely impossible in their mindset.

Isn't it just like God to wait until something is completely impossible in man's mind before He brings a breakthrough? It's like that old show business saying, "It ain't over 'til the fat lady sings." With God, it's never too late.

It's Too Soon to Give Up

This story gets better. Stick with me here. Jesus was about to teach His friends, Mary and Martha, and His disciples how to "shift their dish." They were all used to shifting their dish toward Jesus as the Healer, as the One Who gives peace and saves. They were about to find out that He is also the Resurrection and the Life. Just because a promise has died doesn't mean it's over, because He's the Lord over life *and* over death. They were about to see the resurrection power of God in action.

This situation required spiritual discernment. One of my preacher friends says, "You cannot get a FM radio station on an AM dial. When you're plugged into the flesh, you cannot understand the things of the Spirit." The disciples and Mary and Martha didn't understand what Jesus was saying because they weren't discerning spiritually. They were looking at the outward appearances and getting caught up in the circumstances. Jesus had said, "This sickness will not end in death." What He actually was saying in the Greek language was, "The conclusion of this matter will not be death. When I am finished, he will not remain dead." Jesus never said Lazarus would not die; He said, "When I get through with him, he will not *remain* dead."

Jump the Facts

This is one of those situations where you have to jump the facts and get real. You may have a promise that appears to have died. You may grieve, but it's still not over. Remember, there is always opposition to a God idea. People may say, "Don't go there. The situation is so bad it stinks." They are the naysayers who look over your fence of life and say, "Well, I told you it was going to happen this way." Sometimes they are almost happy when it doesn't go the way you said it would go. Then they say, "Well, it could have happened if you hadn't done this." Or, "If you'd done it this way, maybe it would have worked out."

> **Your life will not end in the death of your dreams.**

The enemy uses circumstances, events, facts and credible people to help those three giants of fear, doubt and unbelief defeat you. One more time they are going to shove that obstacle in Jesus' way and one more time, He's going to push it aside and say, "It's still going to be all right."

God has already answered your prayers. Your life will not end in the death of your dreams. If they're God ideas, you're one step from a promise, from becoming who you are supposed to be. You must get out of the realm of the flesh and into the realm of the Spirit to see what is happening. Don't expect your God idea to be accomplished your way. God is going to do it His way. It may look impossible, but don't forget the God factor because Jesus is the resurrection and the life. The worse the mess, the greater the message that comes out of it.

An Attitude of Gratitude

In the midst of your mess start thanking God, not for the mess but for the promise. You may have naysayers talking behind your back and a TV news crew knocking on your door for an interview, but keep thanking God that He has already answered your prayers and prepared your comeback. Don't let the enemy take away your loud voice, your shout, your joy, the skip in your step or the glide in your stride. When your faith is in Him, you keep shouting, standing and walking strong.

Sometimes it doesn't look good in the natural, but remember we walk by faith not by sight. When things look dead, is when God is maneuvering things in the supernatural for a resurrection. That's when your miracle is in motion. Don't worry about what it looks like, keep your eyes on THE REFUGE — Jesus. Let me tell you a story about one of the greatest things that ever happened to me.

> **In the midst of your mess start thanking God, not for the mess but for the promise.**

A Miracle in Motion

I was 22 years old preaching at the City Church in Stockholm, Sweden, giving it everything I had, using a lot of energy. After a few days a nice older couple invited me to come to their home in a small village for a rest. I had been speaking throughout Sweden and I was tired. This little village of approximately a thousand people was about eight hours from Stockholm.

I settled into my room in their cozy home and decided to take a nap. In my sleep I heard a voice say, "Get up, get on a bicycle and ride. You're going to help someone." Whenever you hear a voice like that, it's important to discern whether it's God, the enemy or you. At first I thought, "It's got to be the enemy 'cause I'm sleepy." But I kept hearing the voice saying, "Get up, get on the bicycle and ride." It was a "do it now" voice, and I knew it was God.

I got up and asked the lady who owned the home, "Do you have a bicycle?"

She said, "Oh, we have a bicycle but it is a very little bicycle for an eight or nine year old."

I said, "You don't have a bigger bicycle?"

She said, "No, only the little one. Why do you need a bicycle?"

I said, "I'd like to go for a ride."

She said, "Oh, ha, ha, you cannot get on this bicycle, it's too little."

I heard the voice again say, "Get on the bike and ride."

I said, "Oh, no, no, I like little bicycles." I was thinking *God, why couldn't You get me a bigger bike or a motorcycle? A Volvo or a Saab would be even better.* To make a long story short, she finally let me take the bike, all the while trying to talk me out of it saying, "Oh, oh, it's so small; we can take you where...." I couldn't explain it to her so I said, "No. I need to get on the bike."

I picked up the bike, walked through the living room, out the front door to the narrow, winding road to go for a bicycle ride to an unknown destination.

I set the bicycle down and glanced back at my hostess who was waving her hands like I was crazy. It was like a slow motion cartoon. I was riding this little bike with my knees almost hitting my chin. The front wheel was wobbling back and forth as I tried to keep my balance. Here I was God's man of power, the brown Oral Roberts-to-be, praise Jesus, weaving down a little country road in Sweden on a kid's bike with my Afro smashed flat on one side from my short nap.

I didn't know where to go. I saw some people on the corner, and I asked them, "Do you have a lake around here?"

They answered, "Oh, yes, we have a lake. You go left."

I followed their directions to the lake. I could hear the gravel crunch as I rode my little bicycle up to the lake. As soon as I stopped, I heard a voice calling, "Hey, you. Are you from America?"

I said, "Yes."

He started motioning for me to come around to the other side of the lake. God was preparing his resurrection.

As I was riding closer to this Swede, I saw he had long hair and two long earrings.

He said, "Hey, man. You like rock 'n roll?"

I was thinking, *God, you woke me up, didn't even give me time to pick out my Afro, put me on a child's bike, to see some guy who likes rock 'n roll.* Now I don't know about you, but sometimes when I wake up out of a deep sleep, I can get semi-moody.

I said, "No. I don't like rock 'n roll."

He said, "I do. I'm a rock 'n roll kind of guy. I love the Rollin' Stones."

I was still thinking, *God got me here to hear this stuff? Maybe it wasn't God I heard. Maybe it was all that sausage I ate for dinner.* Stick with me. It's about to get good.

He said, "What are you doing here in this dead village, man?"

I said, "I'm here resting."

He said, "Well, what do you do?"

My attitude was going downhill fast, and rather sarcastically I said, "I'm a minister. You know, a bringer of good news."

That's when he screamed, "Ahhhh!"

I said, "What's your problem?"

He said, "I'm a backslider." I was feeling real moody by now and I said, "A backslider."

I wanted to say, "So, what!" That's how disgruntled I was. But he was about to get resurrected.

He said, "Yeah. I'm a drug addict. I shoot heroin. I used to serve God. I was a Pentecostal." He was only nineteen years old.

I said, "That's the kind of preacher I am, a Pentecostal." As I began to talk, God began to get my attention. His power began to flow in me — the anointing, that burden-removing, yoke-destroying power of God that even resurrects people from the dead. I said, "What do you want to do?"

He said, "I wanta, I wanta come back to Jesus."

I saw this little chain around his neck inside his shirt. I said, "Let me see what's in there." He pulled it out, and it was an upside down cross, a satanic cross. I said, "Get rid of that." He threw it in the lake. He threw his beer and cigarettes in the trash can and got down on his knees. I never even asked him to do it. I got off my tiny little bike, laid my hands on him, and the resurrecting power of God shook him and shifted his situation. It only takes one touch to shift your family, your body, your finances or to turn everything in your life around.

He began to weep. I was weeping, the power of God was there. I didn't care if I was riding a little kiddy bike. I didn't care if my Afro was going this way or that. I didn't care if I was missing my nap. I was just excited.

He said, "Now, we must tell my mother-in-law. She's afraid of me. I'm mean to my wife. I'm a bad man. I mean really bad. I must tell her what's happened. The house is right over there."

I said, "Okay, you run and I'll ride."

He ran like Carl Lewis, and I was riding like who knows who. I've been in thirty-eight countries, and I've preached in some of the greatest churches in the world, but what happened next was one of the most wonderful things I've ever seen in my life.

He ran and opened up the door to his mother-in-law's house. There was a living room and a kitchen in the front of the house. His mother-in-law and his wife were in the kitchen cooking. As soon as he opened the door, the mother-in-law took one look at me and started screaming, "Tim Storey. Tim Storey. Tim Storey." I froze in my tracks. You've got to understand, I was a twenty-two-year-old evangelist and hardly anybody knew who I was. I'd never been in this place which was eight hours away from the church in Stockholm where I had preached.

She was still screaming, "Tim Storey, Tim Storey." He ran in, hugged his wife, hugged his mother-in-law. They were all talking in Swedish and crying. They started twirling each other around in the living room. I was standing there and didn't know what was going on. Finally, the mother-in-law spoke in English and said, "This is what happened. I was visiting my sister in Stockholm for a few days. I was at City Church sitting in the back row of the balcony when you were there. As you were preaching I said, 'God, send a man like Tim Storey with his energy, his humor, his boldness and his youth. That's the kind of person it will take to set my son-in-law free. Send someone like Tim Storey.'"

The Bible says, **The effective, fervent prayer of a righteous man** (or woman) **avails much** (James 5:16 NKJV). When that mother-in-law spoke that prayer, the heavenlies began to shake. In the natural the situation looked dead. Her daughter had married a man who had gotten her pregnant before she was married. He was messed up on drugs and beat her and abused her.

This mother feared for her daughter but loved enough to pray for her son-in-law. She saw a young, dark preacher from Los Angeles, California, and prayed, "God, send someone like Tim Storey." God put it in the heart of an older couple to invite Tim Storey to their little cottage to rest. God nudged me to take a nap, woke me up, put me on a little bike and took me to the lake where this messed up young husband was sitting. Isn't our God awesome?

Go Meet Your Miracle

God knows exactly where you are. He can resurrect you out of your circumstances just like He did that young man in Sweden. He has already prepared the pathway for you, but you have to cooperate with your comeback.

Three things that will sabotage your comeback are self-pity, pride and condemnation. Self-pity is when you hear yourself saying, "If you had to go through what I've been through, Mr. Happy-go-lucky, you wouldn't be singin' and dancin' either."

Marilyn Hickey says when we are in self-pity, we nurse it, we curse it, and we rehearse it. We nurse it by constantly feeling sorry for ourselves. No matter what happens our first reaction is "poor me." All of the emphasis is on the "me." Then we curse it with the words we speak out of our mouths like, "My whole family is suffering from alcoholism. I

> **Three things that will hinder your comeback are self-pity, pride and condemnation.**

wouldn't be this way if it wasn't for them. It's all their fault." Then we rehearse it by playing the videos of our past mistakes over and over in our minds. The more we think about it, the more we feel sorry for ourselves.

How many of you could relate to Peter's reaction when Jesus warned him that Satan was going to test him? He was so quick to say, "Not me, I'll never deny You, Lord." Did it sound familiar? Pride, pure and simple, is one of the major stumbling blocks to a comeback. I travel all over the world, and I can't tell you how many times I have heard people say, "I didn't think I would do it, but I did." It happens in all areas of life. We're all capable of it. Let's read what THE MESSAGE says about this in First John 1:8-10.

If we claim that we're free of sin, we're only fooling ourselves. A claim like that is errant nonsense. On the other hand, if we admit our sins — make a clean breast of them — he won't let us down; he'll be true to himself. He'll forgive our sins and purge us of all wrongdoing. If we claim

that we've never sinned, we out and out contradict God — make a liar out of him. A claim like that only shows off our ignorance of God.

> **Be quick to confess sin, repent and go on.**

Be quick to confess sin, repent and go on. God forgives and remembers your sin no more. He's not going to stick around and listen to you rehearse it over and over. That's condemnation, another hindrance from the enemy, to keep you from your comeback. If Peter had said, "Hey, man. I'm a man who failed and I've got to pay. What I did was just too bad. Jesus can't forgive me," he would have been denying God's promise of forgiveness and never fulfilled his destiny. Condemnation comes from the enemy not from God.

Get Up and Show Up

Another important key to your comeback is that you've got to show up. Suppose Peter had been so humiliated by what he had done that he had run away and never returned to the other disciples? The moment Peter heard the rooster crow, he knew he had sinned. He didn't run. He didn't deny his sin. He was humbled and his heart was broken. He was changed forever. It was a new Peter who was in the upper room with the other disciples after the resurrection. Proof of Peter's comeback was when he showed up at Pentecost, preached the sermon of his life and became a great leader.

You've got to show up for your comeback. Even when you're in the middle of a setback and don't feel like it, go take a shower, brush your teeth, change your clothes and quit watching "All My

Children." Erica is doing the same thing she was doing five years ago and still hasn't won an Emmy for it! I don't care how bad you feel, get out of that bed. Look outside and thank God for the blue sky if nothing else seems right. Get up, show up and cooperate with your comeback.

In a little village in Sweden where I was to preach in a church of 65 people over 650 showed up. I was walking through that little village before I even preached and a lady grabbed me by the arm and said in broken English, "Who are you?"

> **Get up, show up and cooperate with your comeback.**

She took me so by surprise I said, "What?"

She said, "I see light coming from your eyes. You are a man of God." This was a charismatic Catholic lady who had never seen or heard me preach in her life.

Another time I was on an airplane. The lady sitting next to me said, "Are you a religious man?"

I was reading *Sports Illustrated*! I said, "Yeah, I dabble in religion on the side."

She said, "Just being around you makes me feel good."

Do you know what she was experiencing? The mercy of God. Mercy that came into my life as I began to cooperate with the comeback that God had planned for me.

Today Is Your Day

That same mercy is available to you, too. To experience it, you simply have to allow God entrance into your life. Allow

Him to encourage you just as He encouraged Peter. Refuse to let mistakes and setbacks send you running away from God. Instead run toward Him. Remember, God can and will resurrect your hopes and dreams. He is the source of your strength. He is the source of your comeback.

CHAPTER 13

MAKING A GOD IMPRESSION

H ollywood is a place where everyone is waiting for their big break. A lot of people have made it big but there are many more who haven't. Back in the late '70s I used to walk around Hollywood Boulevard, witnessing to the prostitutes and the pimps about Jesus. They joked with me and said "Reverend Ike, get out of here." Many of these people came from small-town-America just to be around Hollywood. It's been such a trap, a place of broken dreams and hurting people.

> I believe God can raise up a generation of people who aren't just radicals but revolutionaries.

God has used me to reach the people of Hollywood with monthly inspirational meetings. I believe God can raise up a generation of people who aren't just radicals but revolutionaries. People who stand for godliness and principles without having to be preachy and square. Some were raised in the church but walked away because it didn't pertain to where they were coming from. But this new generation is standing up and saying, "I am a Christian and I am real. I've been in the pit, I got through the storm, but everything is still going to be all right."

Miracle in Motion

Hunter Tylo, one of the most beautiful and talented television stars, testifies that a few years ago she looked great on the outside with a promising career, a beautiful house, a handsome husband, gorgeous clothes, but on the inside she wasn't happy. In reality her career and marriage were in jeopardy.

Hunter and her husband, Michael, found hope and new direction for their lives in the messages from my monthly inspirational meetings and from my tapes. Their lives were transformed and their marriage strengthened. Michael says patience has entered his life, a virtue he didn't have. They discovered the missing link to being satisfied to the depths of their souls. That link is Jesus.

Recently Michael and Hunter have been challenged by setbacks that might have overwhelmed or even destroyed them in the past. Hunter was fired from her role on the television show, *Melrose Place*, because she was pregnant. She stood by her convictions regarding the sanctity of motherhood and sued the producers of the show. This setback could have ended her career, but God had her comeback already prepared, and the lawsuit was settled in her favor. This was an important decision not just for Hunter but for other women facing such pressure in the workplace.

The Tylos are making a God impression, and it has stirred the enemy's anger against them. In January '98, Hunter and Michael were blessed with a second beautiful little daughter. This precious baby has been diagnosed with a rare form of cancer that threatens her eyesight and her life. With the revelation they now have and the strength of the Lord, Hunter and Michael are walking through this valley. They are stretching and growing in ways they never thought they could. God is moving them to a higher level, and they're going to make it. They know that no matter how tough the circumstances appear to be, their comeback is already prepared. Their miracle is in motion.

No Place to Run

Hollywood celebrities have their struggles, but it is no easier for people who are raised in the church, especially if they are a preacher's kid. Sometimes they have to go through the pit and the desert before they find their own way on God's pathway. Their journey is no less painful than yours or mine just because they come from a famous family. In fact sometimes it may be more so. But God has a plan for everyone's life and He is capable of using each one in unique ways to accomplish His goals.

In his autobiography, *Rebel With a Cause,* Franklin Graham shares his personal struggles with growing up as the oldest son of the famous preacher, Billy Graham. From the moment of his birth, people (not his family) put impossible expectations on this boy's shoulders to measure up, automatically assuming he would walk in his father's footsteps. Franklin was not to be so easily led by people or God, and he took everyone on a merry chase for many years. He ran harder than most and didn't learn lessons easily, but he couldn't outrun God.

Franklin loved the outdoors, was inquisitive and adventuresome. Mechanical things intrigued him and as he grew older he developed an insatiable desire for speed and danger. He challenged every motorcycle, car and airplane to perform beyond its limits. This resulted in numerous near-death experiences including more than one plane crash. He always seemed to be doing something that took him right to the edge of disaster.

> **Franklin challenged rules and authority with all that was in him.**

As a teenager, he pressed his luck with a local policeman one too many times, outrunning him in his latest jalopy, speeding through the gate at his parent's home and closing it in the policeman's face. Franklin loved jokes and he laughed as he ran upstairs to his room.

When he heard his father's voice calling him downstairs to face the music for his deed, Franklin wasn't sorry for what he had done, just sorry that he'd been caught. That's when he learned that his father would not defend him or fix it when he got into trouble and was wrong. If the policeman had arrested him, his father would have let him pay the price for his recklessness. Being Billy Graham's son had given him some advantages up to this point but it was a fact, people expected a higher standard from him because responsibility comes with privilege. His father and the policeman made a God impression on Franklin that day.

Franklin challenged rules and authority with all that was in him. Cigarettes got a hook in Franklin at a very early age as he followed around the carpenters who built their home at Little Piney Cove and began smoking their discarded cigarette butts. Alcohol drew him under its wing in college. His relationship with God was superficial, and he truly was a cynic, a critic and a skeptic. Because of this, he faced many setbacks including breaking his ankle in a motorcycle accident, being expelled from high school and college, crashing a rented airplane and other such experiences and failures. But God used every one of these setbacks in shaping Franklin's comeback.

Many of the adventuresome excursions Franklin took to various parts of the world were actually God's preparation for his destiny. He was Billy Graham's son but he was also God's son, and God watched over Franklin, protected him and let him run his rebellious course until it was time for him to step into his own destiny. Franklin would be the first to admit that throughout those years there were many, many people who made a God impression on his life, shaping him and molding him into the man of God he is today.

Franklin's roommate in college was an older, but godly man who helped to watch over and subtly encourage Franklin in the ways of God. This was a man who was focused, who walked his Christian talk, who loved to have fun as long as it was "clean fun" and who shared a love of the outdoors and flying. He proved to Franklin it is possible to walk uprightly with God and not be square or stuffy about religion.

Roy Gustafson, an associate with the Billy Graham Evangelistic Association, took Franklin under his wing and hired him to help with tours to the Middle East during summer breaks from college. Roy's guidance and nonjudgmental advice were a stabilizing force in Franklin's life. The tours to the Middle East spurred Franklin's interest in a hospital project in Mafraq, Jordan, that opened his eyes to how God meets BIG needs in impossible circumstances when believing faith is activated.

> **The divine appointment that changed Franklin's life forever was when God sent a "hit man" after him by the name of David Hill.**

The divine appointment that changed Franklin's life forever was when God sent a "hit man" after him by the name of David Hill. He was an expert in the art of running from the Lord and rebellion. David had been to the doorsteps of hell, and he didn't intend to go back. He would say to Franklin, "Kid, you're running from the Lord. You know you're going to have to get right with God sometime, otherwise alcohol is going to do you in someday." Franklin knew David was the real McCoy and not a phony, but he wasn't ready to change yet.[1]

Two years later Franklin was in Lausanne, Switzerland, helping with some of the logistics of the International Congress for Evangelism sponsored by the Billy Graham Evangelistic Association. He knew there was an emptiness in his life that wasn't being fulfilled with all the adventures he had experienced.

It was time for his father to make a God impression on his life. His parents had never forced religion on him and had given him unconditional love. After going to lunch with them during the conference, he was walking with his father who said, "Franklin, your mother and I sense there's a struggle going on in your life. You're going to have to make a choice either to accept Christ or reject Him. You can't continue to play the middle ground. Either you're going to choose to follow and obey Him or reject Him. I want you to know we're proud of you, Franklin. We love you no matter what you do in life and no matter where you go. The door to our home is always open, and you're always welcome. But you're going to have to make a choice." He patted Franklin on the shoulder and didn't say anything more as they finished their walk. The clock was ticking on Franklin's personal hour of decision.[2]

A few weeks later God used David Hill to speak the Word from Romans 7:18,19,21,23 to Franklin and the words came alive for him. It was like the apostle Paul had read his mail. For the first time Franklin understood that sin was ruling his life and he had no power, in and of himself, to do anything about it. He thought he was a Christian, after all he was Billy Graham's son, but he knew he was a sinner who had been running from God.

After several more days of studying the Bible and hearing his father's words replay in his head, "Franklin, you are going to have to make a choice to accept Christ or reject Him," he got on his knees. He confessed his sin to the Lord, asked forgiveness and invited Jesus to come into his life as Lord and Savior. This rebel had finally found THE CAUSE, and he was through running.

God had Franklin Graham's comeback well prepared. He had been shaping him for years and orchestrated his comeback carefully over the next few years. God didn't change Franklin's personality or gifts. He is using Franklin's adventuresome spirit to take Samaritan's Purse Ministry into some of the most needy and dangerous places in the world, delivering humanitarian and medical relief but most of all bringing the light of Jesus to those who are hurting and dying.

Seedtime and Harvest

There is a time and a season for everything in our lives. There is a time to plow the ground, a time to plant the seed, a time to water the seed and a time to reap the harvest. The frustrating thing is knowing what season we are in. Too often we want to reap the harvest before we plant the seed.

> The toughest trials, tests and tribulations come right before your breakthrough.

When there is opposition to your God ideas, reaching your destiny, you must not get weary. The toughest trials, tests and tribulations come right before your breakthrough. My momma used to say trials come in threes. Now it seems like they come in three dozens! But no matter how many trials come, it's too soon to give up because your comeback is on its way.

God *Always* Shows Up!

In the Bible in the book of Exodus we see Moses going through such a test. He's on the backside of the desert working for his father-in-law. He's been wandering and wondering in this wilderness for forty years, and he's frustrated at being in there for so long. Like the clay pot sitting on the potter's shelf, he's saying, "God, where are You? Hello, God! I'm in the wilderness. Did You forget me? Have You forgotten the God plan in my life?"

You've been there: "I wonder if this guy is for me?" "I wonder if I made the right decision in buying this house?" "I wonder when I'm going to get my big career break?" "I'm tired of going through the same dilemmas over and over." "I'm tired of nursing my problems, cursing them and rehearsing them. God, I want You to disburse them and reverse them."

God shows up in a burning bush, and says, "Moses, take off your shoes, this is holy ground. We're going to have a conversation here. Moses, I have a God idea for you. I want you to make a God impression in Egypt. I'm sending you to Pharaoh to bring My people, the Israelites, out of there."

Too many people lose their self-confidence when they wander for a long time. Moses was no exception. He says to God, "Who am I to go to Pharaoh and bring the Israelites out of Egypt?" It's when we feel the least that we need God the most.

God says, "Moses, I've got the plan, everything is going to be all right. You're going to lead three million people out of Egypt and through the wilderness."

Moses says, "Let's get real. I'm not the guy I was forty years ago. Man, You should have asked me to do this forty years ago when I was in my prime. I was lifting weights at Gold's Gym. I had my attitude down. I was into my motivational tapes, and I'd been through a cleansing thing. I was happening. I was on the edge. But now You're catching me at an awkward time. I'm a little undone. Surely You don't want me now. It's past my time. I'm just not ready."

It is amazing how God calls us to do big things when we don't feel ready. He waits until we are emptied of ourselves and filled with Him. That's when He truly gets the glory. There's nothing of us in it.

> ...God calls us to do big things when we don't feel ready. He waits until we are emptied of ourselves and filled with Him.

Have you watched the Academy Awards and seen stars giving their acceptance speeches say they want to thank God, and then they name everyone else in the universe? What they are saying is it sounds good to include God in the picture but they really believe their own talent and everyone else around them actually made it happen. If they were really giving God all the glory, they would say, "Truly, out of my heart, it had to be God." It's that time in your life when God does things that you know only He could do, because you were in a setback when He pulled you out.

So God says to Moses, "I've got this plan for you to lead three million people...." Moses interrupts and says, "For real, I'm telling You the truth. I'm not the guy I used to be." God says, "Don't worry about it. I *will* be with you." That is a promise you can hang your hat on!

When I was a little kid, a bunch of tough kids lived in one area of town. Every time we went through that area, those tough guys who were older made fun of us and harassed us. I had a friend who owned a pit bull, and one day I said to him, "You know those guys over there on the corner who are always bugging us, let's take the pit bull when we walk through there the next time." Sure enough, when we walked through with the pit bull nobody bothered us. We felt protected.

Never Alone

In the realm of God when you are fulfilling His plan, making God ideas happen, you're not doing it by yourself. He's right there beside you. When you're making big decisions, He's there guiding you. God doesn't call you to a mission and then say, "All right, figure it out yourself." What would have happened if He had told Noah, "Build a boat. I don't

> **God doesn't call you to a mission and then say, "All right, figure it out yourself."**

know how you're going to build it. Just do it!" No. It was His plan and He gave very specific instructions how it was to be built. Do you think Noah could have built such a boat and rounded up all those animals by himself?

God's Assignments Are Bigger Than You

Have you ever noticed God's assignments are bigger than you? He's placing a demand on your life, but you're not to worry. When God gives you an assignment, He will always tell you how to do it and then give you the strength to see it through. He allows you to feel awkward because then you say, "I think I need God."

Moses said, "I don't know how I'm going to pull this off."

God encouraged him and said, "I AM is with you and I'll give you a sign. When you have brought the people out of Egypt, you will worship Me on this mountain."

But Moses was still nervous and said, "Suppose I go to the Israelites and tell them the God of their fathers has sent me, and they ask me what His name is? What shall I tell them? I mean, get real, God. I've been out of the business for forty years. I haven't done any networking in so long I don't have any contacts. They would laugh at my resume, and I don't have a press kit. If I tell these guys, 'God sent me,' they're going to say, 'Who do you think you are?'"

God always has an answer to counter our excuses. He said to Moses, "Don't sweat it. Just say I AM sent you." God went back to His resume and said, "I am the God of Abraham, Isaac and Jacob." In other words, "Ask those guys if I was there for them." He was also saying to Moses, "Didn't anyone tell you what I've been up to the last forty years while you've been wandering around in the wilderness feeling sorry for yourself?"

Lean on Him

> God prepares the pathway for you in advance. He doesn't send you on "cold" calls...

God prepares the pathway for you in advance. He doesn't send you on "cold" calls, as a salesman would say. He qualifies the calls and sets up divine appointments for you. That's why it is so important to learn to lean on Him and let Him direct you onto the path He has already prepared.

Have you ever heard people say, "It's lonely at the top?" I've talked with a lot of people on top — in business, in show business, in ministry — and they all say it is a lonely walk. They are constantly asking themselves, "How am I going to sustain this? How am I going to keep up my image?" They aren't sure who they can trust, and more often they don't know anyone else who they think can relate to where they are. The bigger your dreams are, the more lonely it is unless you are leaning on God. Here's what the Bible says about this.

Trust in the Lord with all your heart and lean not on your own understanding; in all your ways acknowledge him, and he will make your paths straight.

Proverbs 3:5,6 NIV

You can't lean on Him unless you know Who He is. If you take a three-year-old child and stand him on a chair facing backwards and say, "Go ahead and fall backwards, I'll catch you," would he do it? Not if he doesn't know you. If you were his daddy and he knew he could trust you, he wouldn't hesitate. A lot of people don't lean on God because they don't know Him and, therefore, don't trust Him.

Pass It On

Moses was questioning his own understanding and knew what God was asking him to do was impossible in his own might. He had to go back and consider what God had done for Abraham, Isaac and Jacob. God always speaks of three generations. He knows how important it is for one generation to teach the next generation and the next. There is great wisdom to be learned and blessings to be passed along.

One of the reasons the American family has been weakened is because families don't live close enough geographically to teach and make God impressions on the up and coming generation. Parents and grandparents often don't see their grown children or grandchildren more than once or twice a year. As a result, we have become self-centered and only think of our own generation. Children no longer respect their elders.

God is a miracle-working God. A miracle is a supernatural intervention in the natural affairs of men like the parting of the Red Sea. He knows how important it is for one generation to share His miracles with future generations. It's the only way the children will know that God is big enough to meet every need and that He is worthy of praise. We must tell them of His power and about His miracles. It builds their faith and trust.

I was in Sweden and was talking with some young kids. I asked them, "Do you ever want to come to America?"

They all said, "Yeah!"

"Where do you want to go?"

"Disneyland."

"Who is in Disneyland?"

"Moosey Pig." (That's Mickey Mouse in Swedish.)

"Have you ever been to Disneyland?"

"No."

"Well, how do you know about Disneyland?"

"The books."

"Is it supposed to be a nice place?"

"Yes, for (that's how they say it) they have the biggest roller coaster in the world in Disneyland."

"Really?"

One little guy piped up and said, "Oh, and it's very happy there in Disneyland, and there is so much games and people. That is my dream to someday go to Disneyland."

Somebody told them or read to them about Disneyland and made a big impression on them, but their thinking is bigger than reality. As you may know, Disneyland does not have the biggest roller coaster, and I can tell you not everybody is happy there when they're standing in that long line waiting to ride the Matterhorn when it's 106 degrees in the shade.

Here's another example. Back in our school days, my best friend, Marty, and I used to go dancing at Dillons in downtown Westwood. (Don't be shocked. I probably saw some of you there, too.) We were 18- or 19-years-old and after dancing, we always went to a place called Tommy's Hamburgers. It was *the* place to go. So what if we had to stand in line forever. At three or four in the morning we were eating Tommy's hamburgers and thinking they were good.

I had a couple of real cute cousins who came to Los Angeles for a visit. Marty and I took them out dancing and then we said, "Man, now we gotta go to Tommy's, 'cause it's *the* place." The girls were excited thinking they were going to get some incredible hamburgers and meet all these great people there. We pulled up in the parking lot and the first thing they saw were the "interesting looking" security guards.

It was cold that night, and we were standing in a long line freezing to death. The girls' teeth were chattering, and they were saying, "These hamburgers better be g-g-g-good!" The guys were making the hamburgers so fast they just threw everything on them. When we finally got our order, the chili and the lard (you know hamburgers can't be good without lots of grease) were dripping off the sides. The onions and pickles were falling out of the bun. My cousin said, "You've got to be kidding. I'm not putting that in my system!"

So we finally got our food, and she said, "Okay, where do we sit?" I said, "Well, actually, we stand." Oh, those girls were not happy. But Marty and I had Tommy's in our system. We just kept telling people how great Tommy's was.

Imagine if we told our children and our children's children how great God is? We would say, "Man, I was drafted into the Marines in the '60s and I had to go to Vietnam. I didn't think I was going to make it, but let me tell you how God saved my life...."

Or we'd say, "I was trying to go to college in the '70s and it was tough. I couldn't pay my tuition *and* the rent, but let me tell you how God provided...."

Or we'd say, "Your momma and I got married in the '80s and we were so excited when we found out your brother was going to be born. Then the doctors told us there was a real bad problem, and he might not make it, but we prayed and God healed him before he was even born."

> **If we tell our children and grandchildren and others around us about God's miracles and blessings, we will make a God impression on them.**

If we tell our children and grandchildren and others around us about God's miracles and blessings, we will make a God impression on them. According to my studies an impression is a sign, an imprint, a mark left to remember something by. If someone makes a good impression, you remember it. When we're called to do great things for God, why don't we have the faith and confidence we can do it? It's probably because no one has made a God impression on us about the great God we serve. Do you know the story of Moses and the Red Sea, of Noah and the ark, of Jonah and the whale, of Abraham and Isaac or of Daniel and the lions?

We need to believe in the miracles of God. We need to receive the miracles of God, and we need to tell the next generation about His miracles. If we don't leave a God impression, they won't believe in God anymore.

We were created in His image. The problem is we spend most of our time trying to make God into our image. What has God done wrong that most Americans won't believe in His power? It's time to stand up for God. We have one life to live. Why be "regular" or "status quo?" This is a new generation. Let's get radical and revolutionary for Him. It's time to make a God impression so people will know Who God is and that His miracles are for them.

CHAPTER 14

LITTLE PEOPLE MAKE BIG WAVES

T he world is made up of all kinds of people — tall and short, fat and skinny, black and white, blue eyed and brown eyed, blondes and brunettes, cool and not so cool. Each one is made in the image of God, and each one is like none other, endowed with unique gifts and talents to be used for God's glory. It is obvious, when you walk down the street and look at the people you pass, that God loves variety. So who are we to limit His plan and destiny for each one? Who are we to judge what is "normal" or "strange" or "not so cool"? We're all normal people who want to live a big life.

> **God loves to...use the least likely people to perform great exploits.**

God loves to confound the wise and use the least likely people to perform great exploits. Throughout history little people in the eyes of man have been making big waves in the kingdom of God. What makes these little people unique? They love God with all their hearts, with all their souls and with all their strength. They walk their talk and teach others how to do the same. They are real and genuine as they do what is right and good in God's sight. God says those who demonstrate that kind of love will prosper and multiply and possess their promised land.

You may be waiting for your big break in life, wandering and wondering when will it ever come. You may be saying to yourself, "I love God so what's the problem?" Loving God isn't enough; you must be walking in His Word as well. That means prospering where you are planted until He says it's time to move on.

Prosper Where You're Planted

In a previous chapter we talked about how Ananias made a big wave by discipling Saul (later known as the apostle Paul) at a time when no Christian in their right mind would have approached him. Ananias had one big assignment in life, and then we never hear from him again. He doesn't end up in Hebrews 11, the great faith chapter. We don't hear about him like Moses with the Ten Commandments, and there isn't any movie made about him. By his obedience Ananias, a little old man in his eighties, impacted the course of history as the apostle Paul rose up to fulfill his destiny in the kingdom of God.

You can prosper right where you are planted and make big waves. Don't fall into the trap of "if only's." "If only I could find the right spouse, then I'll be happy. If only I had a different job, then I'd be happy. If only we had 2.5 children and a dog named

Spot, then we'd be happy." When you live in the world of "if only's," you are putting off happiness. Take happiness right now and just pull it into yourself. Embrace it and be fulfilled today.

Make some big waves even if you're working at Taco Bell. Help someone where you are, stir their gift, and you may change history. That young man working beside you at Taco Bell may be the next Smith Wigglesworth. Remember the story about the jailer in Philippi praying for salvation with Paul and Silas after the earthquake opened the cell doors? He became the pastor of the great Philippian church to which Paul wrote a whole chapter in the Bible. Don't forget God ideas bring God results.

Think Big in Small Places

Too many times we become so "I" centered waiting for the big break, we are blinded to what opportunities are staring us in the face. It's time to think big in small places. What you make happen for someone else, God will make happen for you. When you open a door for someone else to succeed, you are planting a seed that will germinate and grow with each word of encouragement, with each helping hand. You are assuring a plentiful harvest in your own life. In other words, don't wait for your ship to come in if you haven't sent one out.

A few years back, my friend Vince Evans, who was playing for the Oakland Raiders, came to me and said, "Tim, we need to start a Bible study for the Raiders." So we started one on Mondays. The first Monday, sixteen guys showed up who didn't look like they wanted to be there. I could read on their faces what they were thinking, "Vince drug us in here, man, and we don't want to be here." I'm trying to be motivational and I say, "Okay, everybody stand up, this is going to be great." Two guys stood and the others sat there like, "Hey, Vince, you didn't say I had to stand. Man, the boy's trying to make me stand, and I ain't standing."

But the more I talked the more I got into their spirits, and things began to happen. Those guys who wouldn't stand up the first time were standing and clapping and cheering. They started dragging in their friends. Before long we would have as many as thirty players at a non-mandatory Bible study on Monday morning. Vince took it a step further and baptized these guys in water, and all kinds of things started happening with the Raiders.

It Only Takes One!

I've said this before, but it's so important I keep repeating it over and over. It only takes one. Now say this out loud, "I happen to be the one!" If you're willing, God will use you to make big

> **If you're willing, God will use you to make big waves.**

waves. In the last chapter we talked about seedtime and harvest which represents God's timing. There was a guy in the Bible named Joseph who was a dreamer. That was his nickname, "the dreamer." God gave him big dreams when he was a young man, but it was years before he saw the fulfillment of those dreams.

When he shared those dreams with his brothers, they thought he was a boastful little brat. They threw him in a pit and then sold him as a slave to a group of wandering traders. He ended up in Egypt, sold as a slave to Potiphar, a wealthy captain in the pharaoh's army. But Potiphar recognized God's favor upon Joseph and made him overseer of his house.

Things went well for a time until Potiphar's wife made a sexual advance toward Joseph who refused her and ran off. The wrath of a woman scorned landed Joseph in prison, falsely accused of attacking her. Again, the prison keeper saw God's favor on Joseph and put him in a place of authority. Wherever Joseph was, the Lord prospered him.

The pharaoh's baker and butler were thrown into prison and placed under Joseph's supervision. They each had a dream, and Joseph was able to interpret their dreams for them. The baker was hanged, and the butler was released from prison and restored to his position, just as Joseph had interpreted. The butler forgot about Joseph until two years later when Pharaoh had a dream and needed an interpreter.

Joseph was brought out of prison, cleaned up and taken before Pharaoh to interpret his dream. Joseph continually gave God credit for his giftings and said, **It is not in me; God will give Pharaoh an answer of peace** (Genesis 41:16 NKJV). Joseph explained there would be seven years of plenty and then seven years of famine. The Lord gave Joseph a plan to share with Pharaoh of how to prepare for the time of famine. Pharaoh also recognized the Spirit of God in Joseph and the wisdom he had. He appointed Joseph to have authority over half of the kingdom.

When the famine hit the land of Joseph's father and brothers, they came to Egypt to buy supplies. The rest is history. Joseph was able to save their lives by bringing them to Egypt.

The dream he had as a young man was fulfilled but not until he was in his thirties.

> **Joseph went from the pit to the prison to the palace, but in all of his journeys, he prospered wherever he was planted.**

Joseph went from the pit to the prison to the palace, but in all of his journeys, he prospered wherever he was planted. He respected the authority under which he found himself and allowed the Spirit of God to shine forth in his life. He kept his attitude right and didn't seek vengeance on those who caused him harm. Joseph poured himself into other people's lives wherever he found himself. He was a man of integrity and purpose. God used him to save his family who was in the lineage of Christ.

There is always a process to go through before a dream comes into fullness. Often that process includes testings and trials (disciplines), because it is necessary to know how to prosper in the pit before you can enjoy the palace. There is a dream inside of you to be a world shaker and a history maker but until your dream comes into fruition, help someone else reach his dream. Start thinking big in small places. Stir up someone else's gift.

Impact Potential

I was playing golf in South Africa, and I didn't like the way I saw the black caddies being treated. I decided to motivate them. One of the caddies, named Steven, was murmuring and complaining, and I said, "Steven, who are you going to help by feeling sorry for yourself?"

He said, "Well, that's easy for you to say, you're from America."

"You're probably right, but we need to prosper where we are planted right now."

Steven was totally unkempt. He had a big Afro and there was grass all over it. I said, "Steven, I'm not putting you down, but we're going to have to do something about you. What time do you get off tomorrow?"

He told me what time, and I met Steven and a few of his friends the next day and took them shopping. I bought them some golf shirts and Nike shoes, took them to have Tim Storey haircuts and gave them some godly motivational tapes.

I said, "Now, you guys are going to do something different here, because if you don't act right, your children are going to act messed up and your children's children are going to be messed up because it goes from generation to generation."

These caddies couldn't believe somebody cared enough about them to buy them new shirts and Nike shoes and get their hair cut. They were totally freaked out. Three days later I went back to play golf, and they had their shirts on. They were struttin' around in their Nikes, and they were styling and profiling their new "do's."

That was several years ago, and Steven now runs his own business. He's still looking sharp and the people around him are looking sharp. That one shopping trip and the words of encouragement which were shared gave Steven a new start, a new heart and a new life because someone showed concern about a young caddie. It only takes one person with impact

...little people make big waves.

potential to climb out of the pit and lift an entire family out of the pit.

That's how little people make big waves. It doesn't happen by standing around waiting for the big break. It happens by putting your hope and trust in a relevant, reliable, credible God because He has your future already prepared. It happens by reaching out and helping somebody else obtain their dream.

Splash in the Puddles

Do you remember when you were little and didn't have much on your mind? You'd go fly kites and chase down the ice cream truck and splash in puddles instead of walking around them. You were happy then. As you latch on to what I am saying, you're going to splash through some puddles in life and make big waves. In that job you don't like, you're going to lead somebody to the Lord and that's going to change their family. There in that very situation you don't like, you're going to help somebody, inspire somebody and change somebody's life.

Here's how it works. You reap what you sow. What you make happen for someone else, God will make happen for you. You may be saying, "Tim, you don't understand the hell I'm going through, I can't help anybody." I'm here to tell you, there is always someone worse off than you. There is still hope, and God is big enough to change your life and the lives of those you reach out to in love.

God Looks for a Small Fry

Do you know why God has to find a small fry to do big things? Because the big shots have their own agenda and don't have time for God. God is looking for servants who will do what their Master tells them to do. It takes a servant mentality to make big waves because God knows more than we do. He's the potter and we're the clay.

...by reaching out and helping somebody else obtain their dream.

God uses me to speak into the lives of famous celebrities not because I'm a big shot but because I'm a willing servant. And do you know who usually gains entry for me into the homes of these famous people? My contacts most often come from the nanny or the yard man or the maid. It's just like the servant girl in the Old Testament, who sent Naaman, the commander of the army of the king of Syria, to the prophet Elisha to be healed of leprosy (2 Kings 5).

Naaman was a big shot, and he was furious when Elisha didn't come out and speak to him directly but instead sent a servant to tell him to go dip in the Jordan River seven times. Again, it was Naaman's servants who convinced him to do what Elisha had told him. When Naaman humbled himself and obeyed the prophet of God, he was healed. This mighty warrior returned and stood before Elisha and chose to follow the one true God. One little servant girl impacted a nation as that army commander returned to Syria.

We need to lay down our own agendas and move into a servant mode. Our society has lost this quality. People don't just walk across

Do you know why God has to find a small fry to do big things? Because the big shots have their own agenda....

the street to help somebody like they used to do. We don't even know who our neighbors are anymore. We're afraid to go borrow a cup of sugar from the person who lives in the apartment next door.

One Scrawny Dude

It only takes one little person to make a big splash in the life of someone else. Years ago there was a revival meeting going on and only thirty-eight people showed up to listen to this famous preacher. He preached his heart out regardless of the small number in the audience. At the end he gave an altar call and said, "Jesus wants to save somebody." They're playing that old hymn, "Just as I am without one plea...." One scrawny dude from Carolina came forward and gave his life to Jesus. The preacher may have been thinking, "Only one skinny kid. This revival is a bust." But that scrawny kid was Billy Graham, the greatest evangelist of our time.

Who have you passed by in the past few weeks that you could have influenced? Who have you missed because you're so caught up in your own agenda? How many seeds could have been planted? Do you hear yourself saying, "But Tim, I'm waiting for my big break?" Do you know even Jesus' disciples were looking for their big break? James and John were saying, "Man, when are we going to get the big break?" And then their mother got involved and said, "When you go to heaven, can my kids sit at Your left- and Your right-hand?"

This selfish "me" thing has been going on for centuries. We all get into it. It's what allows people to watch somebody die in the street and not lift a finger to help. I want to tell you where it comes from.

There were three top angels in heaven. For real, it's in the Bible, and this was before *Touched by an Angel*. Of the three top angels, one was Michael, the warring angel (and it wasn't John Travolta!); one was Gabriel, the messenger; and the other was Lucifer, who was the choir director of heaven. He was so beautiful, he was covered with jewels

> We need to lay down our own agendas and move into a servant mode.

and diamonds and rubies. According to scholars, Lucifer was the closest angel to God Himself; while Michael was busy warring and Gabriel was passing out messages, Lucifer stayed in the heavenlies. He was the anointed cherub which means he was the one who covered the heavenlies.

Where It All Began

Right here is where we see that selfish "me" mentality enter in. Lucifer decided he didn't like playing second fiddle to God. In Isaiah 14:12-15, five times Lucifer says, "I will be greater than God Himself." What got into this beautiful angel's spirit to want to overthrow God Himself? Pride and jealousy were what drove Lucifer and caused him to be cast out of heaven along with one-third of heaven's angels who followed him. He wanted the glory, wanted to take credit for everything God did and wanted to be worshipped above God.

It's that same pride and jealousy that have created the dog-eat-dog society in which we live today. That same spirit keeps us

> **Who have you passed by in the past few weeks that you could have influenced?**

from acknowledging that we need God or from admitting that the great things we accomplish are by His might not our own. That same spirit prevents us from loving anyone more than we love ourselves which destroys every precious relationship in our lives. It's the same spirit that keeps us living defeated lives.

The good news is that what Lucifer wanted badly enough to rebel against God for, we have. Jesus gave us His glory, which means to be held in the highest esteem, when He died and rose from the grave.

And the glory which You gave Me I have given them, that they may be one just as We are one.

John 17:22 NKJV

The Bible also says, we are joint-heirs with Christ (Romans 8:17), we are seated with Him in heavenly places (Ephesians 2:6), we are no longer just a slave because God is our Daddy and we can call Him "Abba, Father" (Romans 8:15).

The Power of Choice

We don't have to keep striving for that big break. We don't have to live in the "if only's" any longer. Lucifer, the fallen angel, is Satan, our enemy in today's world, but he is a defeated foe. Jesus defeated him at the cross, and when Jesus rose from the grave He gave us back the authority that was stolen from us in the Garden of Eden. We have the power to choose whether to live defeated lives or to stand up for the things of God. We can choose to live selfish, "me-centered" lives or choose to be the one who helps someone make a big wave in God's kingdom. When we submit our choices to God's purpose and plan, the enemy has no power to work through our wrong choices. So choose to be the person making big waves for God. Be the person who says, "God, let me be the one!"

We have the power to choose whether to live defeated lives or to stand up for the things of God.

CHAPTER 15

FOLLOW THE YELLOW BRICK ROAD

J ust like Dorothy and her friends in *The Wizard of Oz* movie followed the yellow brick road to find their way to Oz where their dreams would come true, you must follow the yellow brick road — priority pathway — God has marked for your comeback. At times that road may seem too steep to climb or too slippery to maintain your footing or too far to travel, but don't allow yourself to be overwhelmed by the journey. Your destination is not always a place, but often it's a new way of looking at things.

> **Your destination is not always a place, but often it's a new way of looking at things.**

We have an enemy in this world, and he is real. His priority is to try to knock you off your yellow brick road or to get you to give up before you reach your destination. It is important to understand you aren't fighting against flesh and blood but against the rulers, the authorities, the powers of this dark world, and against the spiritual forces in the heavenly realms (Ephesians 6:12 NIV). When you feel a heaviness in the city, it isn't just smog.

You have spiritual enemies whether you want to believe it or not. Just because you can't see them doesn't mean they aren't there. It was no different in Old Testament days when the king of Syria sent 3,000 troops to chase down the prophet, Elisha, and his servant (2 Kings 6:8-23). Two against three thousand, that's how life feels sometimes.

Impossible Odds?

Now you've got to realize these Syrians are bad dudes. Nobody wants to mess with them. They cut off folks' arms and legs just to watch them suffer. They are sore losers, too. Elisha has been getting the Syrian's battle plans from the Lord and sharing them with the king of Israel. So this king of Syria is out for blood. He finds out where Elisha is and sends his army at night to surround the city.

When Elisha's servant wakes up in the morning, looks out the door, and sees the city is surrounded by thousands of enemy troops, he runs in to Elisha in a panic and says, "Oh, my lord, what shall we do?"

Elisha says, "Don't be afraid. Those who are with us are more than those who are with them."

The servant replies, "But there are three thousand of them with chariots and spears, and they've got a totally mad look on their faces. Man, I told you we shouldn't have come against these people. Now they're out there with spears and ugly weapons. I don't see anybody else who's going to help us."

Elisha chuckles, "Hey, it's going to be all right. I'm telling you. Those who are with us are more than those who are with them."

The servant lets out a long sigh, "Okay, but you and me against three thousand doesn't make sense."

Elisha prays, "Oh, Lord, open his eyes that he might see." The young man's eyes were opened, and he saw the mountains full of horses and chariots of fire (angels) all around Elisha.

Resurrected Eyes

We have natural eyes, and we have supernatural eyes. We are so accustomed to looking with our natural eyes, we are blinded to the spirit realm. This is where we need to find a new way of looking at things. We need to see from God's eye view, through resurrected eyes. Don't let the fear of your circumstances blind you to God's supernatural solutions.

> **Don't let the fear of your circumstances blind you to God's supernatural solutions.**

When you are feeling overwhelmed, don't fix your eyes on the obvious. Remember, God did not bring you this far to leave you. **The plans of the Lord stand firm forever** (Psalm 33:11 NIV). He is faithful to all His promises. If God gives you a God idea, He's not lying, He's not teasing, He's not fronting, because everything He says is "yes and amen."

Angels on Overtime

Psalm 91:11 NIV says, **He will command his angels concerning you to guard you in all your ways.** So, right when you think you are all alone, God says angels have been commanded to guard you; not just one angel but hosts of angels; not just in some of your ways but in *all* of your ways. When you consider all the stuff you've gone through, don't you think there was at least one angel working overtime on your behalf?

I think some of you work your angels really hard. I'll bet there are some "worn-out" angels from all the *stuff* you've put them through — trying to find the right person, trying to get rid of the wrong person, trying to get the right job, trying to get free from an addiction, trying to lose weight. The Bible talks about angels over 6,000 times. Don't you think maybe God meant for us to know there really are angels, and they're there to protect us and help us stay on our priority pathway — the yellow brick road?

One Step at a Time

> **Restoration comes one step at a time as you build on the momentum.**

Hard times can either school you or rule you. Smart people learn from their mistakes. It doesn't happen overnight. Restoration comes one step at a time as you build on the momentum. Here's a story that proves this better than any example I can give you.

Isaiah Robertson played football for the Los Angeles Rams and was an eight-time All Pro. I think he was one of the greatest linebackers of all time. When I was a kid, I loved watching Isaiah, number 58, play football.

There came a time when all the glitz and power of living in the fast lane took Isaiah from the top to the bottom in life. Drugs got a hold on him and he lost everything he had. But when he hit bottom, a little ray of hope hit him. He knew it was the God his mother had told him about that he had never served. This tarnished hero turned to God and gradually, one tiny step at a time, Isaiah found his way back onto the yellow brick road.

This is the best part of the story. Ten years later, Isaiah has a home outside of Dallas with 65 acres. It's a drug and alcohol rehabilitation home for teens, and they have graduated over nine hundred young champions for God out of that place. Isaiah followed the yellow brick road all the way to his comeback, and he is quick to say, "I would never have become completely this, if I hadn't gone through some of that!"

God is a comeback kind of God. When one of God's children is being restored, the heavenlies see from a different perspective than man does. That's exactly what we need to do. When the obvious seems overwhelmingly negative, it's time to reach out for one more miracle and give someone a hand up.

There is always one more miracle left. Michael Jordan is going to take his last jump shot someday. Evil Knievel had his last daring stunt. Evander Holyfield will fight his last fight. Frank Sinatra sang his last song. But God will never have His last miracle because He was, is and always will be a miracle-working God.

> **When the obvious seems overwhelmingly negative, it's time to reach out for one more miracle.**

New Mercies

Supernatural intervention of God into the natural affairs of men is what you need when your back is against the wall, when you are one step away from your comeback. Life will try to tell you, you've had enough miracles, enough mercy, enough grace; you've messed up on God so many times, you shouldn't even be here. But there is so much mercy in God, He wrote a whole chapter about it in the Bible (Psalm 136). His mercy endures forever. His mercies are new every morning (Lamentations 3:22-23). That's why He never runs out of miracles for us.

Elisha looked up to God and said, "I've got 3,000 mean warriors and one scared servant, I need a miracle, God." God came through. Did you know God even brings miracles in clusters. Elisha learned about God's miracles from his mentor, Elijah who had 14 miracles in a row. Maybe you haven't had one in a long time, so get ready for 13 more. God can overwhelm you with miracles.

That's too Much!

My son, Isaiah, likes Sony Play Station games, especially the football and basketball games. I have a friend who works for Sony, and he gives me the Play Station games whenever he can. I came home one day with a bag of new games, and said, "Isaiah, you've been blessed again."

He was so excited, he said, "Dad, what'd you get, what'd you get this time?"

I said, "Oh, I think there's at least one blessing in this bag. Let me just see what I've got." But I already knew I had eight different games in the bag. I just played it like maybe I had one and said, "Whoa, look at this, MB Live '97."

Isaiah was jumping up and down and said, "Cool, that's just what I wanted."

I strung out the suspense and said, "Whoa, look at this John Madden football...and look at this, Speed Racer...look at this, Motorcycle Racer." The more I gave him the more excited he got.

He said, "No, no, no, no." Then he jumped up and ran around the room in his pajamas and said, "That's too much; that's too much. Stop! That's too much!"

That's the way your heavenly Father wants to bless you, until you're saying, "Stop! I can't take the blessings anymore. I don't even know how to respond. I'm not used to being this blessed." You'd better learn how to become miracle minded, how to get in the receiving mode.

Some of us have been plow minded for too long. Here's what I mean. The law of the harvest says you plow the ground, you plant the seed, you water the seed, and you reap the harvest. Some of us have been so into plowing, we've forgotten we're going to get a harvest. There's a harvest breaking out here, and we're so busy over there plowing we don't even see it.

> It's time to get miracle minded, break-through minded.

Being plow minded is when everything is breaking out around you, and you're still saying, "I just feel stupid; I feel too dumb to do that; I feel unwanted, I feel...." It's time to get miracle minded, breakthrough minded.

Reach To Receive

We've got to learn to reach out our hands and be receivers. Did you know that when you refuse to receive a blessing from someone, you are blocking their harvest? When you refuse the seed from their hand, they can't reap a harvest. Don't get plow minded and forget the harvest.

Another thing we need to stop doing is complaining in the middle of our breakthrough. Now don't get holier-than-thou on me, we've all done it. I remember back in my Bible college days when nobody would invite me to speak. I dreamed about being able to speak to crowds. Then when it finally happened and all the responsibilities became burdensome, I started complaining, "What a drag. I've got to fly 22 hours to get to the Philippines and then try to speak to 20,000 people. I'm tired. This is too much." I'd complain on the plane. I'd complain about the hotel. I'd even complain on the platform. Of course, I'd make a joke of it, but I was still complaining. We've all been there. It's a privilege to do what God has called us to do, and we complain.

I was in Baltimore to speak at a big convention. They put me in a beautiful suite overlooking Camden Yards, the new baseball stadium. I love sports so much and I was saying to myself, "Oh, that's where Cal Ripken is going to hit tonight." I was visualizing the whole thing. I was hooked up. I was walking around in a cushy robe. I ordered room service, but I was grouchy as all get out. I was mad because I was over-worked and stuff was going on and things weren't happening my way. The robe didn't fit right. Then it hit me. I was complaining in the midst of my breakthrough. Look where I came from. There weren't any robes in our house. We had never heard of room service, and the only view we had was of a trash can. I had a case of the "I, ME, MY'S" syndrome.

You know exactly what I'm talking about. You've cried and moaned about getting the right husband. Then you get one, and you complain because he doesn't pick up his socks; he didn't give you the right present for your birthday; he forgot to take out the garbage this morning. Or maybe you've tried and tried to lose twelve pounds. So you lose thirteen and someone says, "You're looking good." Instead of saying thanks, you proceed to say, "Yeah, but I still feel fat, just look at these hips." That's being plow minded. It's time to get miracle minded.

Elijah was the prophet in the Bible who had 14 miracles in a row, but he still went through *stuff* just like you and me. Elisha saw Elijah under the tree complaining and wanting to commit suicide (1 Kings 19). He heard Elijah say to God, "I've had enough." And God said, "Hey, eat some food and sleep a while, you're going to be better in the morning." He saw when Jezebel and Ahab were after Elijah. Elisha saw his mentor when he wanted to give up, and he saw him reach one more time for a miracle.

One More Miracle

The staff who travel with me see me in all types of situations, publicly and privately. I want them to see the entire picture so they can learn from it all. Elisha learned from Elijah, and one day he was faced with a servant who came back with a bad report saying, "Man, Elisha. I think this is the end, but we've had a good life. It was cool. We'll probably end up in the Bible. This is it, man. I'm serious. There's a lot of ugly, mad guys out there looking to kill us. It's totally over now."

That's when Elisha was able to say, "Go up one more time, dude." Then he said, "Now God, do me a favor, resurrect this young man's eyes so he may see the way I learned to see." You've got to learn it and learn it and learn it until you get it inside you. Don't look at the obvious, look through resurrected eyes and reach up for one more miracle.

I love what my friend, T. D. Jakes, says, "You'd better get ready, get ready, get ready, because things are going to start sprouting, something's going to break out, someone's going to break through, a harvest is coming." That's the miracle-working God we serve.

Stick to the Bricks

God is indeed a miracle worker. And He has paved your road with promises. Real promises that you can stand firm on. Promises like Malachi 3:10, **I will...open the windows of heaven for you and pour you out a blessing, that there shall not be room enough to receive it.** (AMP) All you have to do is stay on the path.

And when you encounter setbacks, remember Jesus championed your cause. He fought your fight, He won your battle. Your job is to press toward that prize day by day, one step at a time, until you reach your destination: Comeback!

CHAPTER 16

COURAGE FOR YOUR COMEBACK

T he final ingredient necessary to complete your comeback story is courage. If you are one step away from giving up in any area of your life, God will give you the courage to go on. If you've wandered off the yellow brick road, He will lead you back onto it.

Did you know that courage is an attitude of the heart? *Webster's New World Dictionary of the American Language* defines *courage* as "the attitude or response of facing and dealing with anything recognized as dangerous, difficult or painful, instead of withdrawing from it." It also says that the root of the word, "corage or curage," refers to the heart or the spirit.[1]

The Hebrew word for courage, "amats," is mentioned in the Old Testament forty-seven times. According to *Strong's Hebrew Dictionary* it means "to be alert (on foot) or mentally (in courage)."[2]

In most Bible examples, courage is mentioned in conjunction with "being strong and of good courage." God speaks this word to His people to fill them with hope in difficult times and gives His promise that He will be with them. When Joshua was going into the promised land, when David was facing adversity, when Ruth steadfastly insisted on remaining with Naomi, when the people of Judah were going into battle, over and over; they were strengthened and given the courage to go and do great exploits. God is the same yesterday, today and forever; and He will give you that same courage for your comeback.

Everyone has setbacks but that doesn't mean everyone has to step back. Draw on the courage from deep within your heart and hold on. In the Old Testament there was a guy named Zephaniah. When you go to heaven, who knows, you may live next door to him. In case he asks you if you read his book, you can say, "Yes, when I was reading Tim Storey's book."

Anyway, chapter 3 of Zephaniah speaks of how God will rescue the lame (those who are hurting and brokenhearted), gather those who are scattered (the backsliders), renew their name (remove the shame) and give them fame (restore their reputation). It also speaks of God's joy when His people turn back to Him. This is exciting. Let's read it directly from the Scripture so you can let it sink into your heart:

The Lord your God is with you, he is mighty to save. He will take great delight in you, he will quiet you with his love, he will rejoice over you with singing.

Zephaniah 3:17 NIV

Imagine that, God Himself singing over you! He is going to quiet the storms in your life with His love. This is a promise for you today, for your comeback, so grab onto it and don't let go.

Let me tell you something. The God I serve has received a bad rap. God isn't down on anybody. He's been blamed for a lot of things that aren't His doing. Many times our own wrong choices and the seeds of disobedience and rebellion we have planted are the true cause of our problems. And what most of us don't understand is that sometimes, it's the

> **He is going to quiet the storms in your life with His love.**

seeds of disobedience planted by our parents or grandparents that sprout up in our lives and rob us of our rightful heritage, because the waves of disobedience always wash up on the shores of tomorrow. But whatever the cause, God has a comeback with your name written on it.

Live By Design

God wants you to live by His design not by default. He has a purpose, an assignment, an agenda, an incredible plan for your life. Have you ever heard the saying, "If you can figure it out, it's not God!" God doesn't do things our way or in our time, because He wants us to trust Him totally, to stop leaning on our own abilities and understanding and to acknowledge Him in our lives. Then He will direct our path and make it smooth sailing. That doesn't mean we won't ever encounter obstacles because we will, but He has given us the tools to sail right over them.

Activate Your Dream Machine

Three components of a successful comeback are — imagination, focus and courage. Often when you are challenged in life, you lose your imagination, the ability to dream big. If you're just going through the motions of life, it's time to activate your dream machine and think big again. If you've been living with four-foot ceilings, it's time for a roof raising and the sky is the limit. If the enemy has backed you into a corner, dream your way out of it.

Three components of a successful comeback are — imagination, focus and courage.

Remember, our God is a God of second chances, He mends broken people, and nothing is impossible for Him. I came across this wonderful story told by Ruth Bell Graham that illustrates this point so perfectly.

He had built for himself a great house on one of the Caribbean islands. It is a thing to behold. Tall rusty iron columns, collected and resurrected with an ingenious homemade device. This Great House is a masterpiece of salvaged materials.

A collector and seller of scrap materials as well as antiques, he was also fascinated with broken bits and pieces of china, dug from his yard. His friends, John and June Cash, laughingly remarked it was the first time they had heard of a yard sale where the man had sold the yard itself. Carefully he fitted and glued the pieces together. Few ever came out whole. They remained simply a collection of one who cared.

When I expressed interest, he gave me a blue-and-white plate, carefully glued together — pieces missing.

"You remind me of God," I said. By the look on his face, I knew I shocked him, and I hurriedly explained.

"God pieces back broken lives lovingly. Sometimes a piece is irretrievably lost. But still He gathers what He can and restores us."[3]

Taste the NOW of Today

There is a popular song that says, "Yesterday's gone and tomorrow may never come, but we've got this moment today." It's never too late to start again. Taste the NOW of today. It's the future you've talked about in all of your yesterdays. What are you going to do with it? Let God stir your heart again. Set your imagination in motion and stop looking

> **It's never too late to start again.**

back. After all, God doesn't consult your past to determine your future.

Focus is an important component of your comeback. Do you feel like there's no clarity in your life, like you're off center, not headed for the bull's-eye? If your answer is yes to these questions, you've lost your focus. If you aim at nothing, that's exactly what you will get. Life has slapped you one too many times and you've lost your inner strength, you can't keep going — your batteries are run down.

Aim for the Bull's-eye

One of the reasons you can't stay focused is because not only have you taken a whipping on the outside, but like many of us do, you've been whipping yourself on the inside. It's a double whammy. You're bewildered and confused, just trying to hang on to survive. I can hear what you're saying, "I just hope I get a job to pay the rent." "I know he's not the best, but I guess he's good enough." It's not good enough to just pay the rent. It's not good enough to get someone who barely loves you. There is still somebody who is right for you. God wants you to have His best, don't settle for "good enough."

> **God wants you to have His best, don't settle for "good enough."**

In time of trouble God will be your strength and deliver you out of *all* of your troubles. He stands close to those who are brokenhearted and wounded or crushed in their spirits. The Bible clearly states this.

The righteous cry out, and the Lord hears them; he delivers them from all their troubles. The Lord is close to the brokenhearted and saves those who are crushed in spirit. A righteous man may have many troubles, but the Lord delivers him from them all.

Psalm 34:17-19 NIV

If you have lost focus because you are overcome with troubles or wounded in your heart and spirit, this word is for you. Hold it in your heart and let Him be your strength.

When you are feeling overwhelmed with life, stop telling God how big your mountains are and start telling your mountains how big God is. You're going to go through many troubles in life, but the key word here is *through*. You're not going to stay in them, you're not going to pitch a tent or build a Hilton Hotel in them, you're going to move on through to the other side, because God is going to deliver you out of them *all*.

Run to THE REFUGE!

Here's what happens when people begin to lose focus. They either run for a refuge — alcohol, drugs, cigarettes, food, a person or a place to hide — or they run to THE REFUGE — God! When trouble hits, where do you run? Examine your place of refuge, that place you seek in the midst of the storm, that place of significance.

David was often in trouble, hiding from King Saul or battling vicious enemies; but he found THE REFUGE.

God is our refuge and strength, an ever-present help in trouble.

Psalm 46:1 NIV

For You have been a shelter for me, a strong tower from the enemy. I will abide in Your tabernacle forever. I will trust in the shelter of Your wings.

Psalm 61:3,4 NKJV

Sometimes we need a place of safety, a haven or place of rest, a secure environment to wait out the storm. I was in Florida a few years ago, and the weather station reported a big hurricane was headed for shore. I was used to earthquakes, but I'd never been in a hurricane. Earthquakes are bad but they just come unexpected, and there isn't much you can do about it when one hits. But hurricanes keep haunting you and telling you, "I'm coming. I'm going to destroy you. I'm going to get you."

I called some friends of mine and said, "This hurricane isn't that bad is it?"

"Oh, it's going to be a big one," was their reply.

"How bad?" I asked.

"Well, turn on the news."

What I saw on TV was enough to convince me to find shelter. Roofs were flying off and stuff was blowing all around. It looked like the movie, *Twister*, minus the flying cows.

Life can be like a hurricane. Things can fly at you and go over your head, and you need a place of refuge. When you run to God, not only will He protect your physical body, He will build you up on the inside. The closer you get to Him, He'll start changing your "want to's" and you won't want to do the things you've been doing that got you into trouble.

That tabernacle, the holy place of refuge in Him is a place of significance. That's where God begins to build you up and tells you good things about yourself. When you're built up on the inside and feeling good about yourself, the things on the outside won't be able to shake you. When David went out to meet Goliath, the giant, he was on holy ground; but his brothers were on the battleground and they were worn out. David was fresh and focused and had a great imagination. That's why David was able to knock a giant down with a little stone from a slingshot and then slay him with his own sword. David was in the place of refuge, in the Lord, and that was his strength.

The world in which we live measures success by what we do or accomplish — how big of a house you own, whether you drive a Lexus or a Mercedes, how fancy your corporate title is, where you go on vacation and so on. We are pressured into a performance mode which we then pass along to our children and their activities: soccer, Little League, gymnastics, figure skating, hockey.

Success or Significance?

We have lost our focus on what is success and what is significance. Our true significance is measured by who we *are*, not by what we *do*. Our hectic, rushing world has it backwards. God is not as interested in what we *do* for Him as much as what we *are* for Him. The makeup of our character on the inside is the measurement of our significance in God's eyes.

> **Our true significance is measured by who we *are*, not by what we *do*.**

God will affirm your significance when you seek Him as your refuge. He'll stir you up and tell you things about yourself, like, "I love you just the way you are, but I love you too much to leave you the same."

We all need encouragement and affirmation. My son, Isaiah, plays basketball. You can't find me on Tuesday nights because I take him to basketball practice, and on Saturday mornings, I take him to his basketball games. I like to drive him and even though he's nine years old, I hold his hand. I put my arm around him. When we watch sports on TV, he's all over me. He's all the way a boy and a phenomenal basketball player. I affirm him with positive words of encouragement every day. He loves his daddy and he loves to be around his daddy.

My daughter, Chloe, is seven and she loves her daddy too; because I affirm her and nurture her. I tell her she's beautiful and smart and that she can make it no matter what. I believe that when a father affirms his daughter, she'll be okay with herself on the inside and won't go looking for love in the wrong places.

> **When you find your significance in who you are in God, you'll be okay with yourself no matter what pressures are coming against you.**

When you find your significance in who you are in God, you'll be okay with yourself no matter what pressures are coming against you. He will give you the strength and the courage to do whatever it takes to secure your comeback, because God's opinion of you makes man's opinion irrelevant.

Your Finest Hour

Sir Winston Churchill was Great Britain's greatest 20th-century statesman. He was best known for his courageous leadership as prime minister during World War II. His career was not without controversy and setbacks. During World War I he was forced to resign from the admiralty which almost destroyed his career. His terms in the parliament were sporadic based on what political views were popular at the time. He was denied cabinet office for ten years during 1929-39. His outspoken manner and bulldog tenacity for what he believed often got him in trouble with opponents, but his insistence on the need for rearmament and his disagreement with Prime Minister Chamberlain's appeasement of Hitler were what caused public opinion to demand Churchill's return to the admiralty when Britain declared war on Germany in 1939.

Churchill became prime minister in 1940 during what he called England's darkest hour after the fall of France and the relentless German blitz on London. In one of his most famous and powerfully rousing speeches, Churchill's gravelly voice was heard on the air waves around the world saying, "If the British Empire and its Commonwealth last for a thousand years, men will say, 'This was their finest hour.'" Seeing Churchill with his cigar and two fingers raised in a "V" for victory, inspired the British to keep fighting. His unwavering leadership and military strategies formed a solid collaboration with the United States and other allies which turned the tide against the Nazi regime ensuring its defeat. In postwar conferences, he helped to shape the map of Europe.[4]

Churchill's greatest strength was his bulldog tenacity — his never-give-up attitude. It often got him in trouble with his opponents, but it saved Great Britain from its darkest hour. You may feel like you are in the darkest hour of your life but now is the time to stand your ground and make this your finest hour. Never give up!

The Power of a Comeback

Let me play a video for you of an exceptional comeback story. This story proves beyond a doubt that God's opinion cancels out man's opinion. I had to dig back in the news files ten years. It's the late '80s and the scandal caused by TV evangelist Jim Bakker has made the world news for months on end as the PTL empire at Heritage USA came tumbling down.

The camera focuses in on a sobbing, disheveled, broken Jim Bakker being transported in shackles and chains into court and then to federal prison to serve a 45-year sentence. Many felt it might as well have been the death sentence for this once dynamic, gifted preacher. At that moment Jim Bakker was feeling the sting of the worst setback of his life, but God was already preparing his comeback.

Fast forward this video to the platform of a Bible college graduation ceremony in Dallas, Texas, on May 9, 1998. The camera focuses on a short-statured man with thin, graying hair standing in a black flowing robe hooded with doctoral colors and wearing the traditional mortarboard hat and tassel. Leaving the podium and moving directly toward the 350 graduates, the man's voice rings distinctly through the auditorium, "Don't get stopped on the way to your future. You are a messenger of the Most High God. Just like a railroad crossing says, 'Stop, Look and Listen' you must have a stopping time with Jesus every single day. No matter how big your God-given goals are, you must take time to be with Him. You are the only one who can stop you. You can only be successful with God as you spend time with Him. Set your goals and write them down but don't forget to put in some stopping time with Jesus."

The intensity of the speaker's voice heightens as he nails down point after point. "God has a plan...We're all preachers in training...God sent Paul to prison to write thirteen books in the Bible...Joseph went from the pit to prison before he made it to the palace, because God had to get Joseph out of Joseph before he could save his family and his nation, the lineage of Christ...The harder the trial is the more God is in it...God isn't interested in your works, He is interested in you...Don't fall in love with the things of this world, fall in love with Jesus."

Suddenly tears choke his voice as his passion and emotions pour out, "The first year in prison started out as hell, but it became heaven as I drew closer and closer to God. The last year in prison was the best year of my life with 5 A.M. daily Bible studies and 20 or 30 men being saved weekly. Hard-hearted men were learning how to love each other and how to bear each other's burdens. Camp Jesup became Camp Jesus."

You may have guessed by now the man giving this graduation address was Dr. Jim Bakker. Who could have imagined 10 years earlier that he would ever stand on a speaker's platform again much less preach a graduation message for a Bible college?

Jim Bakker's comeback was unique in many ways. He lost everything he had in the world except his children and his Jesus. He had nowhere to go but up, and God had his comeback already prepared. In God's eyes his future was a clean slate. Jim's life bears no resemblance to the opulent prosperity of the past, and he wouldn't have it any other way. He is currently living in one of the worst ghettos in this country, inner city L.A., ministering to the "down and outers" of his neighborhood and working side by side with his son, Jamie, who has his own comeback story from drug addiction, anger and depression.

That May morning in Dallas, Texas, the audience was awestruck as the power of God's mercy and grace shone through a humble servant from that graduation platform. Tears filled many eyes as the audience witnessed how God had taken a devastating mess and turned it into a miraculous message of redemption for His glory. God always has time for one more miracle.

Jim Bakker went into prison a broken man faced with a 45-year sentence and the hell of surviving prison life. Jim's inner man was weakened by not spending time with God. His focus had been broken by all the pressure of trying to *do* things for God. By striving for success, he had lost his significance. When Jim sought THE REFUGE, Jesus built up his inner man and gave him the strength and courage to endure the isolation and hard prison life.

God didn't hold Jim's sins against him. Jim may have wandered off the yellow brick road for a time, but God had his comeback prepared even before it happened. He applied the pressure of the potter's hand to work out the imperfections, then He took him through the fire. The refining is evidenced in Jim's testimony and the power of the anointing upon him.

Jim's immediate reply was, "Jesus, Jesus, Jesus!"

I met with Jim recently and he blessed my socks off. He is a changed man. His focus is on his Jesus and his courage is undaunted as he ministers in one of the most dangerous inner city ghettos anywhere. The people are drawn to him because of the love of Jesus they see in his eyes and in his heart.

When he was released from prison on parole after serving five years of his 45-year sentence, a news reporter asked, "Jim Bakker, what were the three most important things you learned in prison?" Jim's immediate reply was, "Jesus, Jesus, Jesus!"

It Can Happen to You

Jesus made a way for Jim Bakker's comeback and He will make a way for your comeback, too. He'll provide the courage, the direction, the motivation and the results. That is His free gift to you.

To start enjoying your free gift from God, ask Him right now to show you any ways you have been living wrong. Next, admit, "Jesus, I agree with you. I have not been living life the way You have chosen for me to live. I need to be healed and restored. Forgive me for my wrong living." Don't make excuses, just do it. Say, "Lord I'm giving you my life today, I want You to change me. I want you to put me on the road to a comeback!"

The minute you say that and mean it, God's mercy and grace will overtake you. His love will flood over and through you. You will be free from the mistakes of the past. Your comeback will be set in motion!

THE EYES OF
A WARRIOR

R ecently, I was invited to speak to the Crow Indians. Out of a nation of 10,000 approximately 1,000 men and women came to hear a minister speak on motivation and how God can change their lives. The gymnasium was packed and people were standing everywhere. I spoke from my heart with a supernatural energy and enthusiasm.

The next day, I was immensely honored as they adopted me officially into the Crow nation. The ceremony was awesome, and I was touched beyond words. They gave me a big hat with feathers, and I wore a vest and real moccasins. They danced their tribal dances and sang Indian songs to the beat of their drums.

The most rewarding part of the ceremony was when they gave me my Indian name. I was wondering what it might be, maybe something like "running mouth!" But they gave me a really cool name, "Warring with Wisdom." A leader in the Crow nation said to me, "When you speak, it's like a warrior comes

out of you. You speak like a man who has been through battles."
I thought to myself, "How right you are."

You see, the wisdom I shared with them and the wisdom I have
shared with you in this book didn't come out of living a perfect
life. It came out of a life of losing a dad at the age of ten, losing a
sister two years later, watching the destruction in my family from
generations of alcoholism, living in poverty, dealing with seeds of
anger and rebellion, being misunderstood and at times mocked
for my beliefs; but choosing to get out, choosing to fight again,
choosing to break through and bust out and come back from
every setback. I can truly say, "I am a warrior." I'm not just speaking
a message, I'm living a message! There's a big difference.

The chief said to me at the end of the ceremony, "Tim, it's in
your eyes. There's a warrior in your eyes. You war with wisdom
like a true warrior who takes back the spoils without getting
blood all over his garments."

As you battle through the setbacks in your life and war with
the wisdom you have gained in reading and applying the life-
changing principles in this book, you will earn the distinction
of being a mighty warrior, a vessel of honor, a champion of
faith. You can do it. It's time for your comeback so don't take a
step back. God has already prepared your comeback so run to
THE REFUGE now.

I don't know what kind of setback you are facing right now
but I invite you to cozy up to your Daddy God. It's like building a
fire on a cold winter night, grabbing a nice warm quilt, curling up
on the couch and saying to Him, "Okay, I admit it. I'm not doing
too good right now, God. I need You to help me. I don't have any

strength left but I know You do." That's when God shows up. The Bible says in Isaiah 40:31 NKJV, **Those who wait on the Lord shall renew their strength.**

You're in THE REFUGE and all of a sudden strength starts to hit you and you think, "Oh man, I feel good." You're sitting, you're standing, you're walking and feeling again. You answer the phone with

> I don't know what kind of setback you are facing right now but I invite you to cozy up to your Daddy God.

energy in your voice. Your face comes alive. You've got some juice inside of you again. Now you're running and you feel like running isn't good enough. Suddenly, He picks you up and you begin to soar, just like the rest of the verse in Isaiah 40:31 NKJV says, **They shall mount up with wings like eagles, they shall run and not be weary, they shall walk and not faint.**

This freaks you out but you keep soaring and you begin to enter into what the Bible says in First Corinthians 2:9 NIV, **No eye has seen, no ear has heard, no mind has conceived, what God has prepared for those who love him** (and trust Him). You're soaring and you think, "How did I get this job; how did I get into this relationship; how did I get this life and this joy; how did all this happen?" God picked you up in the midst of a pit and caused you to soar. Once you experience this kind of soaring you won't ever want to step back again, because success breeds success.

You may not be exactly where you want to be, but you can thank God you aren't where you used to be. You're growing and evolving into His masterpiece, winning the battles of life. And

> **You may not be exactly where you want to be, but you can thank God you aren't where you used to be.**

don't ever forget, your comeback story may be the life vest that saves someone else who is drowning in a setback. As you let others see the warrior in your eyes, they will know their lives will not end in the death of their dreams, one step from a promise, never becoming who they're supposed to be. You can be the one to make a difference in their lives, to awaken their hope, to teach them how to dream again, to raise the roof on their expectations. Reach out and touch someone today. They will be changed and so will you, not by what you say but by what you are, God's masterpiece.

Endnotes

Chapter 1

[1] Bourke, p. 32.
[2] Wulf, p. 24.
[3] Ibid.
[4] Ibid.

Chapter 2

[1] *More Stories for the Heart*, p. 25.
[2] Reeve, p. 62.

Chapter 3

[1] Webster, Vol. 1, p.446

Chapter 4

[1] Patton.
[2] *The C.E.O.'s Little Instruction Book,* p.7.
[3] Ibid., p.78.

Chapter 6

[1] Maxwell, p. 76

Chapter 7

[1] Ziglar, p.39.
[2] Microsoft Encarta Lombardi
[3] CMG Worldwide Website

Chapter 8
[1] Webster, Vol. 2, p. 1166.

Chapter 11
[1] Sherman, p. 12.
[2] *Ibid.*
[3] *Ibid.*
[4] *Ibid.*
[5] *Ibid.*, pp. 11,12.

Chapter 13
[1] Graham, p. 117.
[2] *Ibid,* pp. 119,120.

Chapter 16
[1] Webster's, Vol 1, p. 338.
[2] *Strong's Hebrew Dictionary,* p. 14
[3] *More Stories for the Heart,* p. 67.
[4] Sir Winston Churchill.

References

Graham, Franklin. *Rebel With a Cause.* Nashville, Tennessee: Thomas Nelson, Inc., 1995.

"Lombardi, Vince," *Microsoft® Encarta.* © 1994, Microsoft Corporation. © 1994 Funk & Wagnalls Corporation.

Maxwell, John C. *Leadership 101.* Tulsa, Oklahoma: Honor Books, 1994.

More Stories for the Heart, compiled by Alice Gray. Sisters, Oregon: Multnomah Publishers, Inc., 1997.

"Patton, George Smith," *Microsoft® Encarta.* © 1994 Microsoft Corporation. © 1994 Funk & Wagnalls Corporation.

Reeve, Christopher. "Christopher Reeve's Decision." *Reader's Digest,* (July, 1998) 60-66.

Sherman, Elizabeth, "Confidence is the Sexiest Thing a Woman Can Have." *Parade, The Dallas Morning News Magazine,* (June 21, 1998) 11-12.

"Sir Winston Churchill," *Microsoft® Encarta.* © 1994 Microsoft Corporation. © 1994 Funk & Wagnalls Corporation.

Strong, James. *Strong's Exhaustive Concordance: A Concise Dictionary of the Words in the Hebrew Bible.* Nashville, Tennessee: Thomas Nelson Publishers, 1984.

Webster's New World Dictionary of the American Language. Cleveland and New York: The World Publishing Company, 1960.

Wulf, Steve. "The Bible Thumper: Evander Holyfield Praised the Lord and Pummeled Mike Tyson." *Time,* 148 (November 25, 1996) 24.

Ziglar, Zig. *See You at the Top*. Gretna, Louisiana: Pelican Publishing Company, 1990.

About Tim Storey

Tim Storey is a uniquely gifted man of God with a dynamic message for this generation. A well-received, articulate communicator, Tim effectively relates powerful insights from God's Word in a warm, enthusiastic style that connects with audiences of all ages and walks of life.

A highly respected motivational speaker at professional athlete's training camps and to the entertainment industry, Tim is making a profound impact on Hollywood through a monthly Bible study known as **The Alternative.** Each month, he delivers a challenging message to hundreds of Hollywood personalities, including actors, producers, directors and other professionals from the media and arts industry.

Tim receives more than 1,500 invitations a year for speaking engagements across America and around the world. Although his primary focus for ministry is in the U.S., his travels have taken him to 45 nations of the world to share the life- changing message of Jesus' love in churches, miracle services, conferences and on college campuses. Tim's bold presentation of the gospel is accompanied with power and authority.

Tim Storey is a graduate of Southern California College with a Bachelor of Arts in religion. His formal education also includes three years at Florida's Southeastern College. He currently resides in southern California.

To contact Tim Storey,
write:

Tim Storey Ministries
P.O. Box 1428
Whittier, California 90609
www.timstorey.org

*Please include your prayer requests
and comments when you write.*